Praise for Joel Kostman
and *Keys to the City*

"Kostman writes in a deceptively plain style, but he achieves the human connectedness of one of his models, Isaac Bashevis Singer. His stories are a celebration of commonplace strangeness. . . . His keyhole perspective on these slice-of-life stories is incongruously funny."
—*The New York Times Book Review*

"These understated episodes are by turns hilariously erotic and terribly sad. The best show wistful chinks of Kostman's own life. He's got the proverbial steel-trap mind, and if at times he might be suspected of embroidery, he should be promptly issued literary license."
—*Entertainment Weekly*

"The slices of life are as abundant and as fragrant as a Broadway deli's pastrami on rye. These are New York kinds of tales. . . . They provide salty, easy, lively city kibitzing."
—*Kirkus Reviews*

"Each of the tales reads like a short story; the style is economical and observant, and the best ones are imbued with a delicate mix of humor and pathos. The chapter titled 'The Goods' features Eddie Cantor's ninety-two-year-old cousin, who has been hoarding the showman's wardrobe for decades. ('You vanna try dem on? You vanna feel like Eddie Cantor?') At first lost and disoriented, he snaps to attention upon seeing Kostman, and at the top of his lungs, offers the bizarre benediction, 'MAY YOU BE SUCCESSFUL . . . IN YOUR EFFORTS . . . TO GET IN . . . TO MY APARTMENT!'"
—*The Village Voice*

"If Kostman is as proficient a locksmith as he is a story-teller, New Yorkers who use his services can feel secure. . . . Some of the anecdotes [are] humorous, others poignant, a few of them downright sad. . . . What makes his book memorable is his unwillingness to categorize, sermonize about or judge those he meets."
—*Publishers Weekly*

"In the time it takes to swap out a key or to pick a lock, Kostman finds every sort of humanity, and every kind of nut. Spare and perfectly detailed, these stories are memorable and, yes, curious."
—*BookPage*

"A rich, quirky look inside private lives at vulnerable moments. These delightful tales are all marked by such winning humility and honesty."
—*The Seattle Times*

"There are a million stories in the Naked City. We could use more storytellers like this one."
—*Buffalo News*

PENGUIN BOOKS

KEYS TO THE CITY

Joel Kostman is a locksmith in New York City. He lives with his wife and two daughters in Brooklyn.

KEYS to the CITY

Tales of a New York City Locksmith

by Joel Kostman

PENGUIN BOOKS

To Dave Weilgus

PENGUIN BOOKS
Published by the Penguin Group
Penguin Putnam Inc., 375 Hudson Street,
New York, New York 10014, U.S.A.
Penguin Books Ltd, 27 Wrights Lane,
London W8 5TZ, England
Penguin Books Australia Ltd, Ringwood,
Victoria, Australia
Penguin Books Canada Ltd, 10 Alcorn Avenue,
Toronto, Ontario, Canada M4V 3B2
Penguin Books (N.Z.) Ltd, 182–190 Wairau Road,
Auckland 10, New Zealand

Penguin Books Ltd, Registered Offices:
Harmondsworth, Middlesex, England

First published in the United States of America by DK Ink,
an imprint of DK Publishing, Inc. 1997
Reprinted by arrangement with DK Publishing, Inc., New York
Published in Penguin Books 1999

1 3 5 7 9 10 8 6 4 2

ISBN 0-7894-2461-4 (hc.)
ISBN 0 14 02.7947 4 (pbk.)
(CIP data available)

Printed in the United States of America
Set in 12 pt. Electra

CONTENTS

Hard Surfaces   1

The Goods   13

Tarzan Finds a Mate   23

Mr. Pacifico's New Life   33

Mint Condition   41

Cracks   49

The Chapel of Love   63

The Meaning of the Word Discount   69

Chickens, Lobsters, Buicks   79

What We Need to Know About Forgetting   89

Story Value   99

The Naked City   111

The Going Rate   119

True Friends   127

HARD
SURFACES

The president's in town and the traffic is unbelievable. I'm stuck out on West Street, watching a line of black clouds move in from Jersey. Out here on the perimeter of the island, you get such a different perspective. There is actually a vista. I can see a thunderstorm approaching. It's a good time for lunch, I think. I make a quick left turn at Thirtieth Street and head for the Market Diner.

When I settle down into a booth, it is ominously dark outside. The waiter takes my order and I open my copy of the *Times* to the page that contains the president's itinerary. I need to know what parts of the city to avoid at what times. Presidential visits create havoc in my life.

Just as the waiter reappears with my food, my beeper goes off.

I'm not sure if I'll ever get used to these interruptions. Before I became a locksmith, when I sat down for a meal, I sat down for a meal. Nothing except a fire could drag me out of a movie theater. I made plans, often in advance.

"Hamburger deluxe," the waiter says, and lays the plate down in front of me. "Enjoy."

"I will," I say. "But do me a favor."

"What's that?"

"Make it to go."

It's raining so hard the wipers are no help. I don't know how I got into this parking space. The sounds of the water on metal are like a Latin percussion section. The Williamsburg Bridge is about a hundred yards in front of me. I can barely make out the Day-Glo orange mesh they've draped over part of it while the repairs are being made. It is such a sick bridge that they almost decided to let it die and build a new one. Instead, they put it on life support and covered the diseased sections in orange.

It's about a hundred feet to the front door of the building where my job is. I sit in the car, waiting out the rain. As soon as it lets up a little, I make a break for it and am only mildly soaked when I get there.

The intercom panel is emitting a loud buzz. I press *12M* anyway. The sound cuts out. That's a sure sign of a short. I remove my finger. The buzz returns. No one responds. I look at the front door. The glass is cracked and there is a hole where a lock used to be. In the lobby, an older woman wearing an overcoat and hat is standing in front of the elevators, crying. Next to her is a shopping cart full of drenched packages.

"Are you all right?" I ask.

She removes her glasses and wipes away tears. She is unable to catch her breath.

"What is it, ma'am? Can I help you?"

"*No trabaja,*" she mumbles.

"What?"

"De elebator," she says. "Iz no work."

Both of the elevator doors have out-of-order signs taped to them. One is dated April 24, with an apology from the management and a promise to have the problem corrected as soon as possible. The other, with an identical message, is dated today, May 10. Below it on the door itself someone has scrawled in Magic Marker, *You walkin up sucka.*

A young, broad-shouldered black man and I carry the old lady's grocery cart up eight flights. Two out of every three lightbulbs are out. There are large puddles on several of the landings. "Gotta walk your dog somewhere," the man says. The smell of urine is strong.

"Yo, *señora*," he calls down the stairwell.

"*Sí*," a weak voice answers.

"We put 'em next to your door. Okay?"

"*Sí*," she says again.

"Okay," he says to me, "be good." He hands me one of my tool packs, which he has carried over his shoulder, and pats me on the back. Then he takes the stairs two at a time.

I put my head down and trudge up to the twelfth floor. The first door I come to is 12C. The next says 12B. I walk in the other direction and see 12G, 12F, 12E, and 12D. The stairway door opens, and a man comes through. He eyes me, then reaches into his pocket and pulls out some keys.

"Can you tell me where 12M is?" I ask.

"No 12M here," he says. He walks past me and stops in front of 12B.

"Excuse me?" I say.

"I said no 12M in this building. What building you lookin' for?"

"Four-thirty-two FDR Drive," I say.

"Well, this is 430. Four-thirty-two's next door. You have to use the other entrance."

I drop my bags and groan. "You mean I hiked all the way up here for nothing?" I ask.

He smiles and says, "Yep. And the elevators are broken in there too." Then he opens his apartment door and steps inside.

"Are you him?" a man shouts.

He is standing at the end of the hallway. A young girl is next to him, holding on to his arm. The man hops up and down and points at me.

"Gloria? I think it's him. Yo, mister, are you him?"

After twelve flights down and another twelve up, I am so tired I can barely talk. My lungs burn.

"Mister. Mister. You're him. Right?"

"Calm down," the girl says to the man. "Here. Stay here." He hops forward and she grabs him by the arm. "Now, I said stay. Right here. Don't move." She talks to him in a gentle voice and places both hands on his chest. She can't be more than twelve. He could be anywhere from twenty to forty.

"Are you Taylor?" I ask.

"Diaz," the girl says. "Mrs. Taylor is our neighbor. We called from her apartment." She holds her index finger up in front of the man's face and says, "Okay. Now he's here. Remember what we talked about."

"Okay, Gloria. I remember," he says. He is shaking his head vigorously up and down.

"What do you remember?"

"What?"

"What do you remember, Papi?"

"I remember, Gloria. I do."

"Tell me what, Papi."

"Don't get too excited. Right, Gloria?"

"That's right. Now, where do you put your hands when you get too excited?"

"In my pockets."

"That's right. That's good. And where are your hands now?"

"Right here," he says and holds them up like a surgeon waiting for his gloves.

"And where should they be, Papi?"

"In here," he says and dramatically dips them into his pants pockets.

"Good. That's exactly right. That's good."

He laughs. With his hands in his pockets, he lightly hops up and down on the balls of his feet and says to me in a much lower voice, "You're him, right?"

The girl knocks on the door to her left and then opens it.

"He's here, Betty. Thanks."

"Okay," a voice from within calls. "Let me know if you need anything, sweetheart."

"Okay."

The girl takes the man by the arm and walks down the hallway toward me. "Our apartment is at the other end." As she passes me, she smiles, then looks away.

"Give him the keys, Glo," the man says. "You have to give him the keys."

"I will," she says.

She stops in front of 12M and again holds her finger up

in front of the man's face. She reaches into her pocket and produces a set of keys. "This is for the top one. It won't open. We tried everything."

"We been here for hours," the man says. "Right, Gloria? Hours?"

"That's right, Papi," she says. Then she says to me, "We have been here for a really long time. We tried to get my brother, but nobody knows where he is."

The door behind us opens and another young girl comes out. She is shorter than Gloria and is wearing jeans with silver beads attached in circular patterns to the legs.

"Who he, Gloria?" she says.

Gloria steps over to her and whispers something.

"Oh," she says, and giggles. "You go to school for that?" she asks.

"Charlene!" Gloria grabs her.

"What?"

"The man's working. He don't need you botherin' him."

Gloria pushes her back into the apartment. As she closes the door, Charlene says, "Bye, Gloria." She stretches out the words.

I try the key in the lock. It jams halfway through the turn. The man is standing with his back flat against the wall to my right with his head turned toward me. He smiles. "Gloria doesn't want me to say anything," he says.

I nod.

"We've been here for a really long time."

"That's a drag," I say.

"Are you sure you're gonna be able to get in?"

"I'm sure," I say.

"You gonna make noise?" he asks.

"I might have to make some noise."

He looks scared and says, "A lot of noise?"

"Your hands, Papi," Gloria says. "What did I say, now?"

"Okay, Gloria."

She talks to him like he's a baby or a scared puppy, and the sound of her voice seems to calm him. I glance over at her, and she blushes.

I reach into my bag and remove some WD-40, my hammer, and a Vise-grips. The man inches away along the wall, keeping his back pressed up against it. I squirt the spray into the cylinder and clamp the Vise-grips onto the key. Then, holding the tool, I insert the key into the cylinder and kick the door while gently turning. After a few seconds, I manage to trip the lock.

"That wasn't so bad, was it?" I say to the man. He nods at me. Gloria is holding on to his arm. I notice that he is shaking.

"It gets pretty loud in these hallways, doesn't it?" I ask. He nods again. I tap the tile wall with my knuckles. "Hard surfaces," I say. "Echoes like crazy."

He lightly knocks the back of his head against the wall. "Like crazy," he says.

"Papi. Don't do that. You'll hurt yourself."

"Sorry, Gloria," he says.

"Are you all right?"

"Yeah, Gloria. I'm all right."

I open the door. The man rushes by me and into the apartment.

Gloria says, "Thank you. Thanks a lot."

"No problem," I say.

"Can you fix it? I mean, if it doesn't cost too much?"

I look into the apartment. The man is in the kitchen pouring himself a glass of water. He gulps it and some of the liquid runs down his chin and spills on the floor.

"Sure," I say. "It's just a broken knob spring. Don't worry."

"Oh, thanks," she says. She steps through the doorway and adds, "You're really nice." Then she hurries into the kitchen. "Let me do that for you, Papi. Here. Sit down. You want a sandwich?"

"Yeah. Gloria. I want a sandwich."

"Okay. Then sit. I'll make you a ham sandwich."

I watch the way she guides him to a chair and cleans him up with a napkin. Then she makes the sandwich and says to him, "Just how you like it." He smiles at her. "You eat now, Papi," she says and comes back and sits on the floor by the door.

"What grade are you in?" I ask.

"Fifth," Gloria says.

"What does that make you, ten?"

"I'm eleven," she says. "But I know I act pretty grown up."

"Yes," I say. "You do."

"Thank you," she says in a tone of voice that somebody taught her.

"You take care of him very well, Gloria," I say.

"I know."

"Do you have anyone to help you?"

She looks back at the man eating his sandwich in the kitchen. Then she says, "Yeah. Sometimes."

We're silent for a couple of minutes, and then she starts singing to herself. She has a very nice voice.

"You like music?" I ask.

"Yeah."

"Who do you like?"

"Gloria Estefan," she says.

"Same name," I say.

"Yeah. Some people think I look like her. You know, you look like somebody on TV," she says.

"Yeah? Who's that?"

"I don't know his name. He's on some show. He's married to a lady who was on that movie last night. I don't know her name either."

"Well. I'll take that as a compliment."

"What?"

"Thanks."

"You're welcome," she says. Then she adds in a little voice, "I think you're better lookin' than him."

At that moment, a tall, skinny kid appears in the doorway, leans up against the frame where I am working and says, "What's up, Gloria? Whatcha doin'? Wanna come out?"

"No," Gloria says.

"Who's this guy?" the kid asks.

"He's fixin' the lock."

He looks at me and says, "You a locksmit?"

"Yes," I say.

He nods.

"You have to go to school for that?"

"Bernard! Leave the man alone."

Bernard waves his hand at her. "I'll be outside," he says and he leaves.

"Boyfriend?" I ask.

"He wishes," Gloria says.

Suddenly there is a crash from the kitchen. The man has dropped a plate. "Papi!" Gloria yells and rushes to him. "Oh, Papi, I tole you to let me do that. Why you always tryin' to do more than you should?"

"I'm sorry, Gloria. I just want to help. I'm sorry, Gloria."

He stands in the middle of the room with his arms straight down at his sides while she quickly sweeps up the pieces of glass.

"Go sit in the living room," she says. "And don't touch anything till I get there."

"Okay, Gloria," he says.

"So how much do we owe you?" she calls to me. Her voice is now flat and businesslike.

"Fifty," I say.

She finishes cleaning up and walks into the living room, where she says something to the man. He removes an envelope from a drawer and I can see them counting out money.

"Give it to him," Gloria says. "Go ahead. Give it to him."

Gloria and the man come back and he hands me some folded-up bills. "Thank you very much," he says. Gloria smiles at me. It is the same smile she gave when I first saw her.

"It's mad about you," she says.

"Excuse me?"

"The guy you look like on TV. The show is called *Mad About You*."

"Oh, yeah. I know that show."

"I don't remember his name."

"I don't either. But I guess I do look a little like that guy."

"You're better lookin' than he is," she says.

"Well," I say, but the man jumps up and down and starts squealing before I can continue.

"Look at it. Count it. You've got to count it."

"Papi," Gloria sighs. She sounds tired. She motions with her hands for him to calm down.

"But Gloria, he's got to count it. Tell him to count it."

She turns to me. "Please count it," she says.

I unfold the bills and they total fifty-five dollars. I look at the man. He is still hopping, a huge smile on his face.

"Thank you," I say. "That's very kind of you."

"Don't mention it," he cries out, waving both arms as though doing a vertical doggy paddle.

"Thanks, Gloria," I say.

She stands at the door and watches me leave with the man in the background calling, "Good-bye. Good-bye. Thank you. Thank you."

I head back down the twelve flights. Outside, the storm has lifted and there are huge ponds of water everywhere. As I hop from dry spot to dry spot, a voice from above calls out, "Hello." I look up. I have to shield my eyes, but I can make out Gloria leaning over the balcony railing. She waves. I wave back.

"I . . . love . . . you," she calls.

I wave again and head toward my car. The orange mesh on the Williamsburg Bridge is glowing in the post-storm light.

THE
GOODS

No one is waiting at the front door of the building. No one is standing inside by the mailboxes. The guy who called and booked the job had said that his neighbor, an old man, would be waiting by the mailboxes.

"I'm sorry I can't wait with him," he said. "I've gotta go to work."

"Is he okay?" I asked.

"Yeah, he's fine. He's a tough old guy. He's just real old. He's been living in this building for like fifty years."

I tap on the window in the door with a key. No one appears on the stairs. It's nine o'clock at night. It's December and it's bitter cold. I lean forward so I can see up to the first-floor landing. My breath makes a cloud on the glass. I wipe it away. I turn to my left. Two people are standing at the corner of Twelfth and University, waiting for the light to change. They are bobbing up and down on their feet. I turn to my right. A girl with long, curly brown hair is sitting in the ticket booth of the Cinema Village Theater. She is smoking a cigarette and reading what looks like a textbook. There are no customers. A *Woman Under the Influence* is playing. I notice the schedule. It starts in ten minutes. The girl looks up at me. She mouths the words, "It's good." Then she goes back to her book.

A young guy with his coat collar turned up heads out of the building.

"Excuse me," I say. "I'm a locksmith. Did you see anyone waiting upstairs? Locked out?"

"There's an old guy sitting on the steps," he says. "But I don't live here. I don't know the people."

"Would you mind if I went up? It's really cold out here."

He holds the door open for me.

"Be my guest," he says.

Two flights up, a very old man is sitting on the stairs with his head in his hands. He looks asleep.

"Excuse me, sir, but did you call a locksmith?" I ask.

He slowly lifts his head.

"Oh, tank God. Tank God," he says.

"Are you Mr. Kantor?" I ask.

"Tank God," he cries. "You vill let me in. Here." He begins to struggle to his feet. "Dere is da dowah."

He holds the banister with one hand and pulls himself up. His other hand is waving toward the apartment on the right side of the landing. I hold his arm. His skin is soft and mushy. He has little, thin wisps of white hair on his head. Like cotton threads. He squeezes my hand and groans as he climbs the remaining two steps. He is frail but mobile. His shoulders sag but his grip is strong. His voice cracks but I understand every word he says. He shuffles across the landing and rests his hand on the door.

"Here," he says.

He is out of breath.

"Now you'll open it for me."

"Have you been waiting long, Mr. Kantor?"

I set my tools down. I notice that there is an outlet right in the hallway. Unusual for such a ramshackle old building.

"For a locksmith," I say. "How long have you been waiting?"

Mr. Kantor taps the door with his fingers. He is not wearing a coat. Perhaps he merely stepped out into the hallway and the door closed behind him.

"Did the door just close behind you and lock, Mr. Kantor? Is that what happened?" I am speaking loudly now.

Mr. Kantor walks away from the door and runs his hands over his head. I remove a shim and try to pop the latch lock open. The door remains closed. At least one of the three locks on the door must be dead-bolted.

"Mr. Kantor? Are all three locks locked?" I ask. "Do you lock all of these when you go out?"

Mr. Kantor stands at the bottom of the stairs leading up to the next floor. He tightens his face muscles harder and harder. He looks like he's thinking. Finally, he turns to me, lifts his arms about chest high, and says in his thick Yiddish accent, "MAY YOU BE SUGGCESSFUL . . . IN YOUR EFFORTS . . . TO GET IN . . . TO MY APARTMENT."

I walk over to him. He is still holding his arms out. I help him sit down on the stairs.

"I'm going to drill the locks open now," I say. Mr. Kantor nods and lowers his arms.

I have to drill all three cylinders in order to open the door. For ten or fifteen minutes, the noise reverberates in the hallway. No one looks out to see what is going on. When I finally open the door, I look over at Mr. Kantor. He is exactly as I found him a few minutes earlier, head in his hands, eyes closed, motionless.

"Mr. Kantor," I call. "We're in."

He looks up and smiles. He stands and comes over to me, clasps his hands onto my arms, and rubs. Then we step inside.

The apartment has two rooms, front and back, with a galley kitchen in between. There are things lying about everywhere. Books, clothes, boxes, letters, utensils, hats, pots, ties, and bow ties. A feather boa hangs from a coat tree. Remarkably, there is no bad smell. Places that look like this almost always have a moldy, rotten odor, but Mr. Kantor's apartment is relatively clean. Chaotic but clean.

"I can't find da odder keys," Mr. Kantor says.

He is rummaging through his dresser.

"That's okay," I say. "I'm going to install new cylinders."

He looks at me blankly.

"I'll give you new keys," I say.

He nods and pushes the drawer in.

"I still vork," he says. "I gotta haf keys. I'm ninety-two. At least I go to vork."

"Where do you work?" I ask.

"In da garmint bizness. Fifty-five years. Tirdy-sevent stritt. My office. My son don wan me dere no more. But I go anyvay."

I begin to install the new cylinders. On the wall next to the door is a photograph of a young man taken years ago. It is a posed portrait. The man is looking slightly off to the side, his head held up, his face set and emotionless. He is wearing a suit and tie. His high collar narrows to a tiny slit, which holds a tightly wound knot.

"Is this you?" I call to Mr. Kantor, who is opening cabinets in the kitchen.

"Vat?"

"This picture. Is this you?"

He walks over to me. "Dat? Dat is not me."

We stare together at the picture.

"Haf you ever heard of Eddie Cantor?" he asks.

"Eddie Cantor? The singer?" I say.

"Da singer. Da actor. Da vaudevillian. Dere vas only von Eddie Cantor."

After a few seconds of silence, I ask, "Is that Eddie Cantor?"

"Of course dat vas Eddie Cantor," Mr. Kantor says.

"He was a great-looking guy."

"He vas my cousin."

"Really? Eddie Cantor was your cousin?"

"Here. Come."

He takes me by the hand and leads me into the back room.

"Here. Help me push."

He leans over and places his hands on the sides of a large trunk, which sits in front of a closet door.

"Wait, Mr. Kantor. You'll hurt yourself."

"Push," he groans. His hands remain on the trunk.

Together we shove the trunk away from the closet door. He steps around and swings the door open. He steps into the darkness and I hear him moving hangers around. I reach over and pull the light chain, but nothing happens.

"Hold dis," he calls.

He hands me a suit on a hanger.

"Here," he says.

It's a shirt.

"Vat a beauty," he says. "Here." Another suit. Then a vest. Finally, he comes out and tugs at my arm. He takes the items from me one by one and lays them out on a bed.

"He gave me all dese. Dere are more inside. He vore da

best clothes you could buy. Da very best. Eddie vas da most refined man I ever met. Feel da goods."

He holds up the arm of a suit. I finger the material. He lifts it and holds it in front of his body. He shakes his head.

"Nobody like Eddie. Here."

He shoves some boxes over with his foot and removes a robe from the wall, revealing a full-length mirror.

"Look."

He holds the suit in front of me and turns my body. He nudges me a couple of feet to the left.

"Now *you* look like Eddie Cantor. Can you sing?"

I turn to him. His eyebrows are raised slightly.

"I'd walk a million miles for one of your smiles," I croon.

He waves his hand at me and says, "Jolson. Eddie vas better. Nobody could sing like Eddie. I couldn't sing, but ven I vore da clothes, I felt like Eddie. I don vere dem no more," he says.

He stares at me then. His eyes have a clearer look and he appears to be thinking about something.

Suddenly he says, "You vanna try dem on? You vanna feel like Eddie Cantor?"

"I don't think so, Mr. Kantor. . . ."

"Go on. Vat do you got to lose? You're still a young man. Dey look like dey'll fit okay."

I look back in the mirror. The suit is brown with blue flecks. It has wide lapels and is tailored at the waist. It smells a little musty, but the material is still soft.

"Okay," I say. "Why not."

"Good. Good."

Mr. Kantor holds the suit jacket for me and I slip my arms in. He moves behind me and pulls the jacket down in the back. Then he smoothes it with the palms of his hands.

"Dere. Now how does dat feel?"

"Great," I say.

"Here."

He hands me a tie.

"Dis goes good vit it. Hold it up in front of you."

I do as he says.

"So. Now you look like Eddie Cantor. Not everybody can say dat, you know."

I turn sideways and look at myself in the mirror. Remarkably, the jacket fits me almost perfectly. I slip the tie under my shirt collar and quickly make a knot. I am not used to wearing a suit. I'm a blue-collar guy. I feel like I'm looking at somebody else in the mirror in Eddie Cantor's clothes.

"I don tink you need to do da pants," he says.

"What?"

"I tink you got da feeling."

He is looking up at me.

"Right?" he asks.

"Right," I say.

"Good," he says.

He walks over to the bed and returns one of the hangers to the closet. I take off Eddie Cantor's jacket. I put it on a hanger and lay it carefully on the bed. Then I remove the tie and place it on top.

"I'm going to finish putting in the new locks, Mr. Kantor," I say. He doesn't respond. He continues replacing the clothes. I walk back to the door.

After a few minutes, Mr. Kantor comes into the front room. He sits on a chair and hums. When I finish, I pack up my stuff and hand him the keys.

"Vat is dis?" he asks.

"Your new keys," I say.

"New keys?"

"For the new locks. I had to drill the old ones. Remember?"

"Oh, yes." He nods. "Locks."

"Can you give a copy to your son? In case you lose your keys again? That way you won't get locked out."

"Yes," Mr. Kantor says. "My son."

"Okay, Mr. Kantor." I turn toward the door and he calls to me.

"Vait. How much do I owe? I've got to pay you someting. You got a bill for me?"

"Oh, yeah. Sure," I say. I take out my receipt book. "Do you have a pen, Mr. Kantor? I left mine in the car."

"Yes, yes, I tink so. Vait." Mr. Kantor leans over the table next to him and examines it. He scans it inch by inch. He moves some magazines and paper clips and then very deliberately picks up a thimble, which he holds out to me.

"Here. Vill dis do?"

I take the thimble and walk over to the kitchen. I open a drawer. Then another. In the third I find a pencil. I write him a bill for ten dollars. I give it to him. He stands and crosses the room to another table. He picks up a book and pulls out of it a ten-dollar bill. Then he walks back and hands it to me.

"You are kind and young," he says. We shake hands. "And your eyes look good too."

"Don't forget to give a key to your son," I say. "They're on the table here." I point to the spot where he found the thimble.

"Sure, sure," he says.

I pick up the keys and put them in his hand. We walk to the door together. I step out into the hallway.

"Thank you, Mr. Kantor. Thank you for showing me Eddie Cantor's clothes. Good luck to you."

He raises his arms in the same fashion as earlier and announces, "MAY YOU BE HEPPY AND HELTY."

I wave. As I walk down the stairs, he is still standing in the doorway with his arms raised, the keys dangling from his fingers.

TARZAN
FINDS
A MATE

It's a little past midnight and I have just returned home from dropping my girlfriend Deborah off at the airport. Late at night is the only time of day I like the way my block looks. There are no panhandlers, the parking lots are all empty, and the constant noise you hear in the daytime from the exiting Lincoln Tunnel traffic is minimized. It almost looks like a real street, a place where people live.

Remarkably, I find a parking space right in front of my building. I sit in the car with the motor running, listening to the radio and thinking about Deborah. We live together. This morning, I thought we were in love. Tonight, I'm not sure if I'm ever going to see her again.

The DJ plays a Freddie and the Dreamers tune. "I'm Telling You Now." I retrieve a long-lost image of Freddie with that ridiculous half jumping jack he used to do. I saw him on *Shindig* when I was thirteen. I loved the British invasion. I wanted a wave of hair on my forehead. I was going to be a Freddie someday, not a locksmith, not a blue-collar working guy.

Suddenly I hear someone across the street yell something.

I look up and a young woman is standing next to a red sports car, her head resting on the roof.

"Shit, shit, shit," she moans, pounding an alternate fist down with each word.

She steps back, her hands on her hips, and looks around as if for a lost child. She has straight blond hair, which hangs down to her shoulders. When she turns to look in the opposite direction, it flies out behind her like a cape. She is wearing tight blue jeans, a yellow shirt unbuttoned down to her cleavage, and black spike heels. She's got on bright red lipstick and gold interlocking circles for earrings. They jangle when she turns her head.

"Oh, shit!" she says again and throws her bag at the car. It's a Porsche.

I shut off my engine and get out. I don't want to scare her, so I call from across the street.

"Excuse me? You need some help?"

She is bending down on the sidewalk, picking up some things that fell out of her bag. She looks up, and for a second, I think she's going to scream. Then she smiles.

"I locked my fucking keys in the car," she says as she stands up. "I can't believe I did this." Her hands do a kind of Betty Boop thing.

I decide that she's Jersey, here for a concert at the Garden. She just has that Jersey feel.

"You're in luck," I say, still from across the street.

She purses her lips and nods. "Why? You gonna take me out for a drink till the tow truck gets here?" She laughs but starts coughing in the middle.

I go to my trunk and remove my car lock-out stuff. A pretty, stranded Jersey girl, with a sense of humor no less, I say to myself. There is something in her face that reminds me of a young Jessica Lange.

I cross the street with my Slim Jim in one hand. It's a thin, silvery piece of metal about two feet long with some notches cut out at the bottom, used to open car doors. I carry it at my side like a sword, like a knight would. In my other hand, I grasp my tool kit. In my shirt pocket is the little leather case that contains my picks, which I bring just in case I run into any trouble.

I step up on the sidewalk next to her.

"*I'm a locksmith,*" I announce. I love these moments when I get to play the hero.

She has a loopy smile on her face, which stays there even as her expression slowly changes. I can smell the alcohol on her breath. She looks at the Slim Jim and then back at my face.

"No shit," she says. "Well, I guess it's my lucky day."

She lays a hand on my shoulder like we're old pals. She squeezes and then leans on me a little. Her head floats around in front of my face.

"You open it up and the drinks are on me," she says in a kind of half-growl.

I peer into the car window and see the keys dangling from the ignition. There are a couple of empty beer bottles on the floor on the passenger side. I look back at the woman. She's got a cigarette going now.

At that moment, from behind us, we hear a long, clear Tarzan call. It's a perfect imitation, lasting about ten seconds, complete with the jungle yodels in the middle.

"Wha' the hell was that?" the woman asks.

She steps out toward the street and leans her head way

back. She looks up at the parking structure that's a block north on Thirty-first Street. I get a real good look at her then.

"That's Tarzan," I say.

She tilts her head to the side, half closes her right eye, and raises her left eyebrow.

"Fren' of yours?" she asks.

"I think he works in the parking structure."

"Oh," she says with a look on her face that says, "That explains everything." Her expression changes to one of mock concern and she whispers, "Should I watch out for elephants?"

She laughs loudly and hops up on the hood of the car. I move to the door.

"Dressed like that, in this neighborhood, at this time of night, I think elephants are the least of your worries."

"You can say that again," she says.

She puts her hands behind her and leans back. Her small breasts press against her shirt. I momentarily think about Deborah. She is short, dark, with huge brown eyes, large breasts, and thick, long brown hair. She's smart and articulate, although generally a very quiet person. The woman in front of me couldn't be more different in appearance. She is as tall as I am with an accent out of a Stallone movie. She looks like a wild, fun-loving gal. Good working-class stock. I wonder what she's like when she's sober.

"So you gonna do your thing or what?" the woman asks.

I hold up my Slim Jim.

"Action," she says.

Some of the foreign cars are harder to do. Except for the Toyotas and Hondas, which open almost like magic. GMs, Fords, and Chryslers were a snap until they started putting a casing around the back of the door cylinder and made it harder to get to the linkage. But there's always a way. Either you Slim Jim it or you pick it or you resort to the good old-fashioned technology, the coat hanger-like metal dowel. It's a last resort, less impressive, but it works.

I dip my Slim Jim into the car door, feeling around. I try different angles, different depths. Nothing happens. She hops off the hood of the car and stands next to me.

"No luck?" she asks.

"Not yet."

It's a hot night. She takes a tissue from her bag and says, "Here. You're sweating buckets."

I wipe my forehead. The tissue smells like perfume. She removes another one and dabs at her neck and chest. She flaps her hand in front of her face like a fan.

"I've got air-conditioning in there once you get it open," she says.

"I'll have it open in a minute," I say. I start thinking about her behind the wheel of the car, and where we'll go.

She rummages around in the bag again and produces a pack of cigarettes. She lights one up, takes a drag, and blows the smoke up toward the sky. I haven't smoked in ten years, but it still resonates for me. How it feels, how sexy it looks, which is why I think people do it. She offers me one.

"No, thanks," I say.

"Sorry I don't have anything stronger." She smiles. I smile back.

She strikes a pose that smokers do. Right arm bent at the elbow, forearm across the body. The left elbow rests on the right wrist and the forearm goes straight up, the fingers at the lips.

I pull the Slim Jim out.

"Harder than you thought, huh?" she says.

"Some foreign cars are tough," I say.

"Can I try?"

"You wanna try?"

"Yeah. Who knows? Maybe it'll be like beginner's luck. It looks like fun."

I don't know why, but I say sure. I slide the Slim Jim through the space between the window and the rubber stripping. She takes the end of it.

"Like this?" she asks, moving it back and forth like a slot machine handle.

"No," I say. "Actually, you kind of go like this."

I take her hand, move it up and down slowly, bobbing the end of the tool slightly from side to side.

"You don't want to do it too hard or you can disconnect the linkage."

"I bet *that's* trouble," she says.

"Yeah, it is," I say. "*Big* trouble."

She laughs like I just cracked a hilarious joke. She seems to be having a great time.

"Okay," she says seriously and makes a funny face. "I'm watchin' out for that linkage now."

Her words are thick and slurred and I'm afraid she's going to tip over. We are doing a kind of Slim Jim tango, dipping in and out and up and down. The car door won't open, but she doesn't even seem perturbed. It's like we're playing a game.

"I going to try to pick it," I say.

"Can I still do this?" she asks.

"Sure. I'll work on the other door."

As I step away, we suddenly hear Tarzan again. It's louder this time. He must be on a lower floor. It's a particularly beautiful call and he really trails out the last note. The woman bends over double and slaps her thighs in rapid fashion.

"I love that," she cries. "That is just fucking fabulous."

"Local color," I say. I take my can of WD-40 and lubricate the cylinder.

"That guy should be on TV or something," she says. "You should get a news guy out here to interview him. He's unbelievable."

I squat by the other side of the car. I insert the tension bar in the cylinder and hold it down with my thumb. Then I work the rake through several times. She starts playing with the Slim Jim again. I can see her body through the car windows.

"No wonder this car cost so much fucking money," she says. "Even you can't get into it."

After a couple of minutes, I'm starting to get frustrated. I say, "I'll be right back. I'm gonna get something else."

I run to my car and remove the metal doweling I bought on Canal Street for this very situation. It's long and sturdy but pliable. I bring it back across the street.

"Here," I say, "you hold this." She lays the Slim Jim down on the sidewalk. I insert a large screwdriver between the door and the body of the car. "Just put a little pressure on it, like this," I say as I push back. "That'll give me room to maneuver."

She stands behind me and pushes back on the screwdriver. I bend the end of the dowel into an *L* and slide it in. I push it toward the button, which is in an impossible spot on the door panel, just behind the handle. I'm thinking, this fucking car *is* a pain in the ass. I wiggle my end of the dowel and poke at the area of the button, but I keep missing.

"How does that button work?" I ask. "Do you push it forward or in or what?"

"Gee," she says. "I don't know. Let me think."

She bobs her head slowly side to side and finally says, "In, I think. I think."

I keep poking at the button. Once I hit it square on and let out a whoop. But when I try the door, it doesn't open.

"Damn!" I yell and slam my fist down on the top of the Porsche.

"Hey," she says. "Come on. We'll get it." She puts her hand on my arm. "You know you're a really sweet guy for helping me out." She leans forward and kisses me on the cheek.

When Deborah said good-bye to me at the airport, she said, "Maybe you and I should take the next few days to reevaluate." Then she put her hand on my upper arm and kissed me on the cheek.

"Let's try it again," the woman says.

"Listen," I say, "I'm sorry. I'm just frustrated. I usually don't have this much trouble."

"It's okay," she says. "I know we're gonna get it this time." She punches the air like a cheerleader.

We try again. I twist the dowel around to get it in just the right position and then push it forward with my hands so it will come smashing into the button. The door doesn't open. I do it again. And again. As my body bumps into the woman's and rubs up against her, I get more and more crazy. I can feel my hero status evaporating.

Finally, after about fifteen minutes, she says, "You know, I think if I push this way with the screwdriver, it'll make more room. I think it'll be a lot easier for you."

Before I can stop her, she leans against the car and pushes.

There's a loud crack. The window shatters into pieces, which fall on the sidewalk at our feet.

I look at her face. Her mouth is wide open, her shoulders raised in embarrassment. Then, suddenly, she opens the door, brushes the glass off the seat with her bag, and gets in.

"Well, I gotta go," she says.

She starts the car.

"I don't know how to thank you," she says and she speeds off toward Eighth Avenue.

"Good-bye," she calls out.

I am stunned by the swiftness of her departure. As I watch her drive off, her hand waving out the window, Tarzan gives his grand finale. His voice is so strong that it sounds like he's right behind me. His call begins with one beautiful, long sustained note. He holds it longer than I have ever heard before. Then he leaps into a spectacular trill, which ends with another gorgeous full note, and follows this with the second trill, which trails off into a final eerie, haunting tone.

I turn to face the parking structure. I am standing in the middle of a pile of my discarded tools and broken glass. I lean my head way back, looking up at the sky. I cup my hands around my mouth, take the deepest possible breath, and yell at the top of my lungs, "SHUT THE FUCK UP!"

MR.
PACIFICO'S
NEW
LIFE

"**W**ho's that at the door? Has the little prick come back?" Andrew Pacifico calls out wildly from the bathroom. He's in the tub. Although I am standing just inside the door of his apartment, I can see him reflected in a mirror hanging on the kitchen wall. He is gripping the sides of the tub and half pushing himself up, like a gymnast doing a routine on the horse. He looks ready to spring out at any moment.

"Relax, Andy." A tall, thin man with silver hair, dressed in a white linen suit, is standing in the kitchen. He speaks to Pacifico through the open bathroom doorway.

"I am relaxed!" Pacifico yells. "Who the hell's out there?"

"It's just the door guy."

"What door guy?"

"Don't you remember? We decided it would be a good idea to change the locks."

Andrew Pacifico slips back down into the water and moans, "Oh, right. I must be losing my mind." Then he barks, "Tell him to be quick about it."

The man in the kitchen removes a glass from the cabinet over the sink. Then he opens a lower cabinet, takes out a bottle of scotch, and pours three fingers. He swallows it in one smooth motion.

"I don't think you should worry about Carlos, Andy," he says.

"Why the hell not?" Pacifico yells again. "He almost killed me."

"Because you should be worrying about yourself," the man says calmly. He refills his glass. "Besides, why would he want to come back, anyway?"

"Maybe to see if I'm dead," Pacifico says. "Or to finish me off."

"Oh, get a grip on yourself for crying out loud. Carlos is gone. For good."

"Yeah. And so are most of my things."

"Objects can be replaced, kiddo."

"Not love objects," Pacifico says. It sounds like he might break down and start sobbing at any moment.

"Oh, please," the man in the white suit says. He turns and approaches me.

"You'll have to excuse him," he says. "The poor guy is heartbroken. His little prick lover left him. Took a lot of money and his favorite cuff links. His nerves are all shattered. So do you know what you're supposed to do?"

"Yes," I say.

"Good. Why don't you take care of it as fast as possible."

"Son of a BITCH!" Andrew Pacifico screams from the bathtub.

It's been twenty-five years since I have seen Andrew Pacifico.

Back then, he was a short, stocky muscular man with hands

KEYS TO THE CITY

that hurt you when he squeezed yours. He had a head full of wild curls and a permanent two-day growth of beard. He paced constantly. He was moody. He would spend the entire period scowling and lecturing us as if he thought we were the greatest burden any intelligent human being could be saddled with, and then suddenly, just before dismissal, he would burst into a euphoric description of how appreciative he was to have the opportunity to enlighten us.

Mr. Pacifico was unlike the other high-school teachers. He was so passionate about literature that it seemed to physically pain him when we students didn't respond in kind. But Mr. Pacifico never gave up trying to pry open our tightly glued adolescent minds.

He was prone to speech making. The speeches were always inspired by something we were reading but quickly took on a life of their own. I still remember one, which ended up being about cellos. "An instrument with dignity," he said. "Put a cello in any musical piece and automatically you have something more than you did before." He brought his own cello in to school and made us listen to the sounds. The tones. He made us close our eyes and feel the dignity floating around his classroom.

The hallway wall in Mr. Pacifico's apartment is filled with photographs of him. Some are publicity shots, scenes from movies or plays. There is one of him sitting next to a famous actor at a table in a restaurant. They have their arms around each other and their heads are touching.

The man in the suit appears, holding a drink. "They worked together on a TV show," he says, lifting his glass toward the photo.

"I remember it," I say.

"You do?" he asks.

"Yeah. He played a private eye, the guy the cops always went to when they needed information from the street."

"That's right," the man says in a surprised voice. "He'll be thrilled. He thought no one ever watched that show."

"Robert?" Pacifico calls from the bathroom.

"What is it, Andy?" the man says.

"Robert. Please come in here."

Robert downs his drink and shakes his head. I am holding a screwdriver. I point it at a photo of Mr. Pacifico in a production of *Richard III*.

"I saw him in this at the Beaumont," I say.

The man crinkles his forehead and looks at me.

"I thought he was great," I add.

"Really?" he says.

"Robert? I'm cold. I need my robe."

I look at the kitchen mirror. Mr. Pacifico is standing up in the tub, shivering.

"I'm coming, Andy. It's all right. It's going to be all right," Robert says.

He walks across the kitchen toward the bathroom.

A few minutes later, Robert guides a robed Andrew Pacifico across the kitchen into the living room. He sits him down in a wing chair at the far end next to the window. Mr. Pacifico is hugging himself.

"Are you warm enough?" Robert asks.

"Why do these things always have to happen at Christmastime?" Mr. Pacifico says.

Robert takes a pillow off the sofa and props up Mr. Pacifico's head.

"There. Is that better?" Robert asks.

"I need a drink," Mr. Pacifico says.

"Do you want ice?" Robert asks.

"Of course I want ice. Only he-men like you drink scotch without ice."

I am finishing my work. I turn my back to the living room because I can feel him staring at me. Could he possibly recognize me? Not a chance, I think. It's been too many years.

"Hey, key man," Mr. Pacifico calls.

I turn to him. He is a bald, paunchy shadow of his former self. Robert hands him a glass. He takes it with his right hand and keeps his left wrapped around himself.

"How safe am I?"

"Excuse me?"

He looks at Robert. "Am I not speaking English here?" he asks. Robert shrugs. "How safe am I?" he repeats. "What's the little prick got to do to get in?"

"Break the door down," I say.

"Not impossible," Mr. Pacifico says and takes a long swallow.

"Andy," Robert says, "you look like you're feeling better. Are you feeling better?"

"Oh, I'm on top of the world, Robert. What time are our dinner reservations?"

Robert buttons his jacket and lifts a coat from the coffee table. He places his hand on Andy's cheek.

"Listen. Kevin's on his way over, but I have to leave right now. . . ."

"What do you mean you have to leave? You're going to strand me here with this . . . stranger?" He calls over to me,

"No offense, key man." Then, "Sit your ass down, Bob."

"Look, Andy. I just talked to Kevin. He's jumping into a cab and he'll be here in five minutes."

"What's so goddamned important you can't nurse me through one measly little breakdown? How many times have I sat with you?"

I fumble loudly with my tools, tossing them back into my bag. It seems more appropriate than feigning invisibility.

"Look, Andy. You're going to be fine. Kevin will be here any minute. Maybe that's him right now."

The elevator door opens and an older couple steps out into the hall. They stop and gaze at me through Mr. Pacifico's open apartment door.

"Everything all right?" the old man asks.

"Fine," Mr. Pacifico calls. "Lock trouble."

The woman tugs at the man's arm and they walk off. Robert goes into the kitchen and deposits his glass in the sink. Then he starts toward the door.

"Robert!"

Robert stops in front of me.

"Where are you going?" Mr. Pacifico yells.

"I have theater tickets, damn it," Robert says. "Kevin will be here any minute. He'll stay with you."

I lift my tool bag and stand at attention.

"I'll call later," Robert says. As he hurries by me out the door, he shoves some crumpled-up bills in my hand.

"This should be more than enough," he says and heads through the stairwell door.

Mr. Pacifico begins to cry. He says something under his breath. Then he starts to sob more loudly. I am holding his new keys. I don't know whether to walk them over to him in the living room or leave them on the kitchen counter. While I am debating, the elevator door opens again.

"Replaced me already, Andy?"

I turn and see a young man standing in the hall.

"Don't come in here, Carlos," Mr. Pacifico says. "If you set one foot in this apartment, I'm calling the police. Close the door. Key man, close the door."

"I left some of my things," Carlos says. He walks into the apartment, pushing by me as he does.

Mr. Pacifico throws his glass at him. Carlos jerks to the side, and the glass shatters on the wall to my left.

"I believe that's my CD player," Carlos says, pointing at the unit across the room. He moves to the far wall. Mr. Pacifico leaps up out of the chair and stands with his back against the window. Carlos reaches behind the shelf unit and begins disconnecting wires.

"And my CDs. Most of these are my CDs," he says.

"Those are my CDs," Mr. Pacifico shouts.

"The hell they are." Carlos holds a warning finger up in front of his face. "I bought them. They are mine."

Mr. Pacifico is shaking now. Carlos hoists the CD player under his arm and walks toward him. Mr. Pacifico backs along the wall into the far corner. Carlos follows and Mr. Pacifico bumps into something, which crashes to the ground. I quickly step forward and see Carlos standing over Mr. Pacifico, who is on his knees sobbing next to a fallen cello.

"You are a little shit," Carlos says. "You are a washed-up, ugly little shit."

"Why don't you just get out of here," I say. I am standing in the middle of the living room now, holding my hammer at my side.

"Who the fuck are you?" Carlos asks.

"I'm the key man," I say. "Why don't you put down the CDs and get out of here."

"They're my CDs," Carlos says.

"Think of it as payment for the damage to the cello," I say, lifting the hammer.

"What's going on here?" a voice calls from the doorway. "Jesus, Carlos. What have you done to him?"

Carlos drops the CDs onto the floor and wraps the cord around the CD player. He heads toward the door.

"Go take care of your little shit friend, Kevin," he says. He slams the door on the way out.

"My God, Andy. Are you all right?" Kevin asks. He rushes over to Mr. Pacifico and helps him to his feet. Mr. Pacifico slumps into the chair.

"It's okay, Andy. Everything's going to be all right. You'll see."

Mr. Pacifico holds his hands up to his face and begins to cry into them.

"I need a new life," he sobs.

I put the keys on the coffee table. Then I walk across the room and carefully replace the cello on its stand. Mr. Pacifico is still sobbing when the elevator door opens and I step inside.

MINT
CONDITION

The elevator smells like piss. Its walls are covered with graffiti. Two withered old Chinese ladies half my size get on just before the door closes. They stand in the opposite corner, chattering. One of them is carrying a plastic bag filled with green leafy vegetables. A large fish tail sticking out of its paper wrapping is wedged between the cabbage and the carrot stalks. The fish and piss odors produce an overpowering stench.

I get off at the eighth floor. A black woman is mopping. As I walk around her, she asks without looking up, "Who are you lookin' for?"

"Mrs. Moody," I say.

"What do you want *her* for?"

She stops mopping and rests her arms on the handle. Sweat is pouring down her face.

"I'm here to do a job for her," I say.

She takes a deep breath. "Well, you're gonna have a hard time doin' that, 'cause she isn't home. She's at work."

"I know. I'm supposed to talk to her neighbor—8D," I say.

"Well, why'd you say Moody, then?"

She dips her mop into the yellow plastic bucket at her feet. Then she grabs the collar on the shaft near the bottom and slides it down, causing the sponge to fold in half, wringing out the excess liquid. A few drops land on my shoe.

"Last door on the right." She points her mop handle down the hallway. This time my pants are hit.

As I walk past her, she says, "It was her damn husband puked all over the place this morning."

There are two drawings taped to the door of apartment 8D. They are both done in crayon and marker. In the one on the left, a group of people wearing multicolored clothing stand in a row. Their mouths are all open. At first, I think they are crying out in pain. Then I realize they are singing. The words *My Family* are written across the top. The other drawing is a map of Africa. Several of the countries are labeled. South Africa takes up one third of the whole map. Somalia is a peanut in the upper right-hand corner. A string of letters attached at each end by a piece of tape hangs in a smile underneath the drawings.

HAPPY KWANZA.

I knock on Libya.

A pleasant-looking, older black woman greets me with a smile.

"Locksmith?"

"Yes."

A skinny kid about ten years old appears next to her. He is dangling a large key ring from his fingers.

"Just follow him," the woman says as the kid scoots past her. "I guess you know what to do."

"Yeah," the kid and I say simultaneously.

She closes the door.

I follow the kid all the way to the other end of the long hall. The woman with the mop is gone. We leave footprints in her work. There is a strong smell of ammonia. The boy inserts a key into the top lock of apartment 8M. It clicks open. Then, one-handed, his fingers find another key and he repeats the process with the bottom lock.

I am there to add a third.

The boy enters. The spring hinges are wound too tight and the door slams behind him. The explosion echoes in the hallway. When I enter, he is in the living room. The radio and the television are blaring loudly. A rap song blends with a soap opera. He holds a remote in his hand and begins channel surfing.

I find an outlet to plug in my drill. I lay out my tools and the parts of the lock I am about to install. Then I check out the door. There is a large dent in the frame just below the level of the knob. Several chips of white paint have been dislodged, exposing a previous layer of purple. The bottom half of the door juts into the apartment. A powerful boot must have done that damage, I think. I'll have to go higher for the new dead bolt. Up to eye level. It's not ideal, but I have no choice. Usually, it's better to space them out. High, middle, low. Makes the assholes work harder.

In the living room, the music is no longer playing. The kid is watching *The Price Is Right*, and the studio audience is yelling dollar amounts at a hesitant contestant.

The kid says something.

"What?" I say. "I didn't hear you."

I step into the living room. His back is to me.

"Three and two to Mattingly," he says.

He is wearing headphones, holding a baseball bat, and announcing his own game.

"Mattingly got good wood on that last one," he says. "Pulled it just foul. Looks like he's in the zone."

The kid chops the bat down several times. Elbows pulled in close to his sides, slightly crouched, a perfect imitation of Don Mattingly's batting stance.

Then he swings.

"He swings," the kid says, "and there's a shot to right center field. Nettles scores. Here comes Randolph. Heeeeee's safe. The Yankees win!"

He bounces up and down on the balls of his feet and high-fives his invisible teammates. I silently return to the door, and begin to cut the cylinder hole. I imagine that the roar of my drill is crowd noise.

I am screwing in the cylinder when the kid slips by me and goes out into the hall. He has removed his headphones but is still carrying his bat. He begins swinging again.

"This is a big pitch," he announces. "He stretches. He delivers. Swing—and a line single to right."

"Big baseball fan, huh?" I call to him.

"Yeah," he says and walks over to the door.

"Who's your favorite team?"

"Yankees."

"It's hard to be a Yankee fan nowadays. You know, with Steinbrenner. He's such a jerk."

"I don't care 'bout him."

"Who's your favorite player?"

"Ricky Henderson. Then Dave Winfield. Then Mike Pagliarulo."

"Pagliarulo's having a tough year," I say.

"Yeah, but he hit more homers than anybody las' year."

"That's true."

"You like baseball?" he asks.

"Yeah. I'm a big fan too."

"Wait a minute," he says and runs past me into the apartment. He returns holding some baseball cards.

"Look at these."

He holds up an old Lou Brock card.

"That's a 1978," he says. "This Tim McCarver is 1978 too. He played for the Phillies then."

"That's *my* favorite team," I say.

"You a Phillies fan?" he asks incredulously.

"Yep."

"How come?"

"That's where I was born. Philadelphia."

He looks at me as though I had said the name of a foreign country. Like Somalia.

"I think people always root for the team from their hometown. Don't you?"

"Guess so," he says.

"Where did you get the cards?"

"My dad and me went to a flea market up near Albany. Paid a dollar each for 'em. Here's a Dave Winfield when he was on San Diego."

"You know," I say, "those cards might be worth something someday. I mean, something big. You should hold on to them. Don't lose them. Keep them in good condition."

"My dad says these are mint," he says. He fingers the Dave Winfield card. "He's gonna buy me a scrapbook for them."

"That's a good idea," I say.

He slips the cards into his shirt pocket and picks up his bat again. He steps out into the middle of the hallway and practices swinging. Every once in a while he says, "Pow."

Just before I finish, a woman gets off the elevator.

"What are you doing, Samuel?" she yells. "You're not supposed to be out here in the hallway playing. You finish your homework?"

"Yes, Mama."

"Well, did you clean up your room? Did you put all those papers away? I'm sure you must have something else to do besides playing out here in the hallway."

The boy walks past me with his head down.

"I'm Mrs. Moody," she says to me. "You almost finished?"

"Yes, ma'am," I say. "I am finished."

"Good. 'Cause I'm on my lunch hour," she says. "God, I hate to have to spend my damn lunch hour doing this."

She steps up to the door and runs her fingers over the outside lock plate I have just installed.

"This gonna make it so he can't get in?"

"It's going to make it a lot harder. Three locks. Steel door."

"Steel door doesn't mean anything to my lunatic husband," she says. "He puts that crack pipe to his mouth, and he turns into a madman. You see what he did here? Would've broke the whole door down if I hadn't opened it."

"Well," I say, wondering if she is really interested in or needs any opinions from me, "at least this will give you a few extra minutes, then. If the guy is intent on getting in or if he's big enough, or has a big enough hammer . . ."

"This man does not need a hammer," she says.

She walks into the kitchen, which is just off the hallway where I am working. She pours a glass of water. "Damn," she mutters and takes a bottle of aspirin off the table. She shakes several tablets out and swallows them.

"Samuel?" she calls. "Bring me that money I gave you."

Samuel appears and hands his mother an envelope.

"And turn off that TV."

The boy walks into the living room and flicks off the television.

She hands me the money and says, "Can you believe that that boy idolizes him?"

Then she turns and walks toward her son but stops halfway. She puts her hands on her hips and just stands there, breathing deeply. She appears to be staring out the window at the Manhattan Bridge.

"He even works for the Transit Authority," she says.

I pick up my tool bags and look over at the kid. He is sitting on the couch. When he meets my gaze, I say, "Keep swinging."

Before he answers, his mother, still staring outside, says, "I will. I will."

The boy is caught in a half-nod, his chin stuck up in the air. He is a little embarrassed. Without saying anything, he removes the baseball cards from his shirt pocket and stares at them as though they are pictures of friends he hasn't seen in a long time.

CRACKS

The door opens a few inches and one dark brown eye peers out at me.

"Can I help you?" a woman's voice whispers.

"Delivery," I say, as I have been mysteriously instructed.

She opens the door quickly, reaches forward and grabs my wrist.

"I'm Mrs. Herzog," she says. "Thank you so much for coming. I can't tell you what a nightmare this has been."

Her face is heavily made-up. She reminds me of an old Joan Crawford with the thick eyebrows, the full, painted lips, the simultaneous presence of toughness and faded sexuality. She flutters her astonishingly long eyelashes.

"Come in," she sighs. "Please come in. But we must keep our voices low."

I step into the apartment. I am standing in a foyer, a rectangular area about five by eight feet with a small table for the mail, a brass bucket for umbrellas, a coat closet, and enough wall space for a mirror and a painting.

"Let me take your coat," Mrs. Herzog says. She looks quickly to her left as though someone had just spoken from the bedroom. I take off my jacket and hand it to her. She moves her head slowly in a circular motion and, after a few seconds, says, "Things are disappearing."

"Really," I say.

"Yes," she says. She hangs up my coat and then turns back and slips her arm through mine.

"Remember. Low voices," she whispers. She leads me into the dining room. "My sister is in the bedroom. Probably with her ear to the door."

She smiles and I see small lines running vertically through the pancake on her cheeks. She is wearing a rose perfume that makes me sick to my stomach.

"I just hate having to do this," she moans. "But it seems I have no choice. First it was little things. Change lying around, a pair of earrings, and then little baubles, things I'd find at a curio shop. I'd leave something here on the table." She rests her fingertips on the wooden surface. "Maybe I hadn't figured out yet where I was going to place it, and the next day, it would be gone. At first I thought nothing of it. Actually, I thought it was me. I'm not young anymore, as you can see, and I tend to be a little forgetful. It didn't really occur to me that she was plotting against me, lifting these things right from under my nose to get back at me, as if I hadn't spent all these years taking care of her."

Mrs. Herzog stops and places her hands on my arm.

"Of course, I would never have resorted to this kind of precaution at the beginning. Not even if I had guessed, not even if I had caught her red-handed. I'm a big believer in second chances. But when it began to happen a-gain and a-gain, well, I guess I'm just the forgiving type. Are you—" She emits a mild gasp and widens her eyes. "I'm so sorry," she says. "I don't even know your name. I can't call you Mr. Locksmith, now, can I?"

"My name's Joel," I say.

"Well, I'm the forgiving type, Joe, are you?"

"I guess so," I say.

"I thought so," she says.

She walks over to the edge of the hallway and peers toward the bedroom. Then she looks back at me and hisses, "But my sister sure isn't."

There is a closet in the dining room. Mrs. Herzog asks me to install a lock on it. She stands a few feet away from me as I drill and smoothes her hair.

"Would you like something to drink, Joe?" she asks.

"No, thank you," I say.

"Oh, I forgot," she says. "If she comes out, which she probably won't, but if she does, just say you're the electrician. Will that be okay?"

"Sure. That's okay."

"You know, on second thought, maybe handyman would be better. Yes, I think handyman, and you're repairing some damage from a . . . water leak. Yes, that's perfect. Because we did, in fact, have a water leak several months ago. The damn fool upstairs left his bathtub running. Can you imagine? Leaving a bathtub running while you go downstairs to buy a paper? He stopped in the lobby to have a conversation with the woman from 12B. She's another story entirely. They're gabbing away in the lobby while I'm getting rained on here in my own dining room. Look"—she points at the ceiling—"there are the cracks."

She lifts my chin with her right hand and traces the lines in the ceiling with her left.

"That reminds me," she says. "I told you about the missing silverware, didn't I?"

"Yes."

She points to the shelf at the top of the closet. It is filled with hatboxes. Some have the letter *B* written on the front in Magic Marker, others the letter *M*. "That's where I'm going to store the rest of it." Her eyes twinkle. "Just let her try to get at it." Suddenly her mouth drops and she swallows hard. She says, "Did I mention the scratch in the dining room table?"

"I don't think so, Mrs. Herzog."

"Just come over here and look at this."

I put my drill down and follow her to the table. Mrs. Herzog bends over and points to a faint line several inches long etched into the veneer. She runs her fingers along it as though it were a human scar.

"My mother gave us this table," she says.

"It's beautiful," I say.

"God rest her soul," Mrs. Herzog says. "I have inherited her burden."

"Mrs. Herzog, I have to . . ."

"Yes, of course," she says. "I'm so sorry. I didn't mean to disrupt your work. Please finish."

I return to the closet. I notice little sprinklings of sawdust on the sleeves of several coats. One is a full-length fur, another wool with a fur collar. I brush the wood shavings off onto the floor.

"I don't suppose it will be easy for anyone to get into this once the lock is on," Mrs. Herzog says. She is holding a plate of fruit and cheese.

"Not unless they happen to be carrying a drill or a crowbar around with them," I say. I measure the frame and make my marks.

"That's good. That's exactly what I need," she says while chewing. She holds the plate up to me.

"No, thank you. Maybe after I'm done," I say.

She takes another piece of apple and bites into it.

"My sister is a very sick woman," she says. "I've been taking care of her for years now. It's soooo tiring. I can't tell you. I can't imagine how our mother did it." She laughs. "Actually, I don't know why I say that. Mother was sixty-two when she died, and I've already lasted longer than that, although God knows how. I guess I've just got a stronger constitution. As sure as I'm standing here, it killed her." Mrs. Herzog wearily shakes her head. "Schizophrenics are no picnic. Have you ever known anyone who was a schizophrenic, Joe?"

I pick up my drill and hold it up to the frame. I keep my eyes straight ahead as I place the tip of the bit on my mark.

"Yes," I say. "My brother is a schizophrenic."

It's a steel frame, unusual on an interior door. It takes about twenty seconds to drill the hole and when I'm finally through and the noise subsides, she says, "Why, then. We have something in common."

When I was twenty-seven, my thirty-year-old brother drove to New York from his home in Washington, D.C., and disintegrated right in front of my eyes, the victim of a violent nervous breakdown. He chose me as his confidant, his crutch, the only human being in the entire world who understood what he was going through. For twenty-four hours,

I nursed his paranoia and kept him alive. Finally, I was able to persuade him to accompany me to our parents' house in Philadelphia. Once there, he reluctantly agreed to let a doctor give him some drugs. Years later, he is still a psychotic shell of his former self, the family's burden. Mrs. Herzog is right. Schizophrenics are no picnic.

I am finished now. Her coats and hats and silverware are safe. Mrs. Herzog is nowhere to be seen, so I pack up my tools and carry them into the foyer. I glance down the hallway to the bedroom. The door is slightly open.

"Mrs. Herzog," I call softly. "All done."

There is no response, no sound from within. I step up to the door and peer through the small vertical opening.

"Mrs. Her . . . zog," I say again. My voice sounds like it does when I play hide-and-seek with my neighbor's young daughter. I reach for the knob. The door is suddenly yanked open and Mrs. Herzog steps out into the hallway. One hand behind her, stiff-backed like a flamenco dancer, she fits herself into the space between me and the door. A finger is pressed up against her lips.

"Sssh," she whispers angrily. Then she pats down the air in front of her. "She's sleeping. It's the only time I get anything done."

"I'm sorry. But I figured with all the noise from the drilling . . ." I say, stepping back.

"Loud noises don't wake her," she says. "It's the little things. Like squeaky doorknobs. You can't imagine what those drugs have done to her brain."

Suddenly her face changes to a look of embarrassment and then to one of compassion. "Oh, but of course you can imagine, Joe," she says. "You know all about these things from your poor brother."

Mrs. Herzog looks at me as if she wants to give me a hug. "Was it bad for you? Like it has been for me? Was it a horror?"

"Listen, Mrs. Herzog," I say, "here are your keys. And here's the bill. You have a good, strong lock on your closet now, so you can store any valuables you want in there. She won't be able to get to them."

"Are you sure, Joe? Are you really certain?"

"Yes, I'm sure."

"Even with . . . *him* helping her?"

"Him, Mrs. Herzog?"

She raises her eyes to the ceiling and motions silently for me to follow her. We return to the dining room, and as we pass the apartment door, she glances at it over her shoulder as though it's alive and watching us.

"Twelve-K," she says, jerking her finger upward. "They're in cahoots."

"I see," I say. "Well, she won't be able to get into it even with *him* helping her."

"Oh, I'm so relieved. Okay, let me get my checkbook."

I watch her walk into the living room. She moves like an ancient runway model, constantly aware she's being watched. When she had opened the door and come out of the bedroom, I had a quick look inside. It was an attractive, orderly room. The shades were raised, letting in the sunshine. I caught no glimpse of a mad sibling.

Mrs. Herzog returns, checkbook in hand, and sits at the table.

"We were so very close as children," she says. "I think that's one of the things that has made it so hard. Were you?"

"What?"

"Close as children."

"No. At least I don't remember it that way."

"Does he?"

"No. Well, I don't really know. Maybe he does."

She opens her purse and removes a pen and something else.

"Here. Look at this," she says. "This is a picture of the two of us at the beach. I was eighteen, and she had just turned twenty. We were quite the pair. Lines and lines of beaus." Mrs. Herzog laughs. "And we each had plenty of them. No sibling rivalry where we were concerned. No reason. We each had our pick." -

She hands the picture to me.

"She had her first breakdown about two months after this picture was taken. Mother used to look at this picture and say to me, 'I can't see anything crazy in that face, in that sweet, beautiful face, dear, can you?'"

The two girls in the photograph are both attractive, not extraordinarily beautiful, but each has a bright, alive look.

"We don't look like sisters, do we, Joe?"

"No," I say. "Not a lot."

"And we never acted alike either." She nods. "She was such a wild one. You see that bag in between us in the picture? She actually kept a bottle of booze in there. I swear. Started when she was fifteen. She drank constantly. When our mother wasn't looking, of course. Even now I find them all over the apartment." Her voice changes and she leans in toward me. "That's when I began to figure out that she had someone working with her." She nods several times. "You know who."

Mrs. Herzog holds the pen over her closed checkbook. I notice that tears are welling up in her eyes.

"He *buys* them for her," she says. "How else would she get

them? She never leaves the apartment. Hasn't been out of here in years. How they met I can only guess." She stands and walks into the living room, where she pulls a tissue from a box on the end table next to the couch. "Probably when I was out shopping," she says, dabbing her eyes. "Maybe he got a piece of our mail in his box. Maybe he needed a cup of sugar. Oh, I don't know. But as sure as I'm standing here, she must have charmed him. Oh, she can be quite the charmer, Joe. Despite her condition. My sister can charm the pants off of someone when five minutes before she was mumbling about creatures hiding in the closet.

"I remember once, Joe, when she was certain, swore to the heavens, that Oprah Winfrey was sending messages to her through the TV. I swear to you, Joe—that was one of her prize moments. She started screaming about how she needed quiet, complete and utter quiet, so she could *receive* Oprah Winfrey's communications. Oprah Winfrey, mind you. My sister can't stand colored people. What was she doing getting messages from one over the television?"

Mrs. Herzog walks across the room and turns. She places her hand on the top of the crimson overstuffed chair in the corner.

"And then, right in the middle of it all, someone, I can't remember who, comes to the door and I open it, reluctantly of course, because there is my sister ranting and raving about receiving secret communications off the television set, and what happens? She just turns it off. Like that. Sits right here, on this chair, as if she had just finished her afternoon tea and smiles, like a sweet quiet little girl."

Mrs. Herzog suddenly glances to her right as if she's noticed a large bug crawling across the surface of the wooden console that stretches along the wall. She walks over a few steps and then slightly adjusts the position of two brass candlesticks.

"Mrs. Herzog?"

"Yes, Joe," she says expectantly. She raises her head and pats her cheeks with the tissue she is still holding.

"I really have to go," I say. "I have other jobs booked."

"Of course, Joe. I'm so sorry," she says. "I didn't mean to—" Suddenly a pained look comes over her face and she gasps.

"Are you all right, Mrs. Herzog?" I ask.

Mrs. Herzog's head jerks several times.

"Mrs. Herzog?" I ask again.

She rolls her eyes to the side. I look to my right and am startled to see an old woman in a wrinkled nightgown standing at the end of the hallway. She has long gray hair that hangs down wildly and partially covers her face. Her feet are bare. She is stooped over and rocks slightly.

"Hello, Sister," Mrs. Herzog says.

The woman reaches down with her right hand and begins to scratch her leg. She starts at the calf and then moves upward, raising the hem of her nightgown until her fingers are digging visibly into her upper thigh.

"This is Joe, Sister. He's the handyman," Mrs. Herzog says nervously. "He's come to repair the damage from the water leak. You remember when Mr. Delgado went out for his paper and left the bathtub running?"

Sister emits a deep lung-rattling cough. She is leaning up against the wall, still scratching.

"Can I get you something, dear? Joe is just leaving. Why don't you go back to the bedroom. I'll write him his check and then we can have a nice lunch."

Sister begins to walk across the dining room toward the

kitchen. She shuffles her feet as though weights were attached to them. I look to Mrs. Herzog. She is shaking her head no. Sister stops in front of me and looks at me with fury in her eyes. Then she abruptly continues her trek.

We stand in silence while Sister opens the refrigerator and removes the milk. She pours herself a glass and replaces the carton. She takes a sip. Then she inches her way across the dining room, down the hallway and back into the bedroom, spilling little drops of white liquid every few feet.

"You've been very patient," Mrs. Herzog says. She hands me a check.

"Thank you," I say.

"Would you like something to drink before you go? A glass of soda?"

"No, thank you, Mrs. Herzog. That's very kind of you."

I lift my tool bag.

"I know I've imposed far too much already, Joe, but could I ask you just one more very quick favor?"

"I really have to go."

I don't have any other jobs booked, but the time I've spent with Mrs. Herzog has worn me out.

"I just need your professional opinion about something," she says. "I promise. It will be very quick."

For about a year after the onset of my brother's illness, I thought I should be his keeper. I even entertained notions of moving back home to Philadelphia, finding a place for the two of us to live, watching over him. Fortunately, I never did act on these impulses.

"Okay," I say. "But please make it quick."

Mrs. Herzog scurries into the living room. She lifts a vase

off a shelf and turns it over. A key falls out. She uses it to open the top drawer of the desk in the corner. She removes a stack of papers and brings them to me.

"Here," she says. "If they figure out a way to get in, and they always seem to find a way, I just want to know which of these items might be appropriate for the front door."

She spreads the papers out on the table. They are copies of pages from a locksmith catalog.

"I don't understand," I say.

"Well, I thought that these two look like my best bets. The Unican 1000-1 and the Corbin Sesamee padlock. What do you think? The Unican looks like a very solid item."

"It is, Mrs. Herzog, but you don't need a Unican. This costs over four hundred dollars. Besides, I can't imagine it will do what you want."

"That's what I was afraid of. That's why my backup plan was to go with this Corbin Sesamee lock. It's got a combination I can change myself and that's really what I'm most concerned about. They are so devious, Joe. It doesn't matter where I hide things. They *find* them. You see where I'm keeping the key to my desk? That's where I'm keeping it today. You think a little old vase will stump them. Not a chance. I have dozens of hiding places all over the apartment. And that's exactly why I thought this lock might be just the right item. I mean, when they get the combination, then I could just change it. Myself."

"Mrs. Herzog, I don't really think you have to do anything like this. You can just keep your valuables in the closet, and you won't have any more problems."

Mrs. Herzog eyes me for a second. Then she says, "No more problems? Are you kidding me? I don't think you realize just how serious a situation I have here. My sister does not rest. She will not be content until she has brought everything down. And I mean everything. This is not something I can sweep under the rug. This is a matter of survival. She brought our mother down, and now she's working on me. No more problems? I don't think so."

I stand there silently, trying to find a response. Finally I say, "Well, I think the Corbin padlock. It's a very reliable and affordable item."

Mrs. Herzog takes a deep breath and walks over to the front door.

"Can I use it with this hasp?" she says, pointing to a piece of hardware installed near the bottom of the lock-filled door.

"Yes," I say. "You can use it with that hasp."

"Good," she says. "Now at least I have a fighting chance."

She walks back to the dining room table and gathers the papers. The photograph of the two girls at the beach is lying there. I realize that Mrs. Herzog never told me which of the two girls she was and that now, even having seen her sister, I would be hard pressed to make an accurate guess.

Mrs. Herzog escorts me out into the building hallway.

"By the way," she says. "Please don't say anything to the doorman about the locks."

I hold my index finger up to my lips and say, "Mum's the word."

"Good," she says. She puts her index and middle fingers together and holds them up in a Scout's honor sign. "Because he's like this with the guy in 12K."

THE
CHAPEL
OF LOVE

"A musician is a peanut," he says.

The musician sits on a chair and talks to me while I work. He is wearing a nicely ironed white, short-sleeved shirt and a pair of green chinos. His hair is black, flecked with gray. It is short and neatly combed.

"Yeah," he says, "nothing but a damn peanut."

He lives in a tiny one-room apartment underneath the Manhattan Bridge. Trains roar by overhead. Sometimes the noise is so loud it is difficult to hear what he is saying.

"I never should have gone to Juilliard," he says. "It really messed up my perspective."

He stands and walks over to the kitchen, which is a sink and a half-refrigerator. There is a hot plate sitting on the counter beneath a homemade shelf on which some cups are stacked next to a few plates. Two saucepans hang from hooks from the shelf.

"You're in your own special little classical world there. It's not the real world. Musicians don't rate in the real world. Took me years to get that straight."

He opens the refrigerator and removes a pitcher.

"You want some iced tea?"

"No, thanks."

He pours a glass for himself. "All I ever really wanted to do was play popular music," he says. "But I was just a kid. What did I know? Julliard was my parents' idea. I came all the way from Hawaii. Luckily, I was smart enough to drop out."

"What instrument do you play?" I ask.

"Guitar. You know what really bugs me?"

"What?"

"Americans can't play Hawaiian guitar. They only copy."

I have already figured out what's wrong with his lock. It will be an easy repair, so I allow myself the opportunity to continue the conversation.

"You know, there was a hit song when I was a kid," I say. "Came out in the fifties. It was called 'Hawaiian Love Song' or something like that. It was an instrumental with the Hawaiian guitar." I sing a little of what I think was the melody.

"Right," the musician says. "Americans. That was typical. The big hit Hawaiian guitar song was done by Americans. Junk. When that song came out, though, there was a lot of work for us. I spent years on the road playing Hawaiian music. Spent some great days in Kansas City. Ever been there?"

"No."

"Great town. I played with some fine musicians. A first-class gig all the way. Didn't last long, though. Harder times after that."

We hear the sound of an instrument coming from outside. The musician frowns and walks to the window. He is stirring the sugar around in his glass. I look too. There is a guy leaning up against a car, playing a saxophone.

"He thinks he can play," he says.

"You know him?"

The musician sips his tea. "Unfortunately," he says. "He wouldn't know good music if he tripped over it."

The sax player looks up and waves. "You almost ready?" he calls.

The musician yells, "B flat." Then he steps back into the room and says, "What an idiot. He makes the same mistake every time."

"I'm almost finished here," I say.

"Take your time," he says. "We're only going to Staten Island. The wedding's not till three. He's not paying me enough to get there early."

I am engaged to be married in two months. My fiancée, Rebecca, and I have hired a classical trio to play at our wedding.

"So are you in a band?" I ask.

The musician laughs to himself. "Not a chance. His guitar player's sick. Every time his guitar player gets sick, he calls me to bail him out."

A train rattles by. The cups and plates shake.

"I'm a bartender," I think he says.

"So you finally ready?" the sax player asks. He is sitting on the hood of the car, holding his instrument between his legs.

"No," the musician growls, "I just came down with my guitar to tell you I'm going to be another twenty minutes."

A group of six kids is standing a few feet away, watching. Two Chinese girls, three early-adolescent black boys, and a little white boy who couldn't be more than five, with a Marine-type brush cut. They look like they are posing for a family portrait, tallest in the rear, the little one in the middle, everyone waiting to say "Cheeeese."

"Friendly guy, huh?" the sax player says to me. "That's the only reason I give him a chance to go on these gigs. Because he's such a nice guy. He can't play a lick."

"Right," the musician says.

The sax player is middle-aged, with a salt-and-pepper goatee. He is wearing a small black cap, the kind Pete Seeger wears, with a snap in the front over the brim.

"Get the lock fixed?" he asks.

"Yes," I say.

He lifts the horn to his lips and begins to play. I recognize the melody—"Goin' to the Chapel and We're Gonna Get Married." I wonder if we can get the classical trio to work up this tune. One of the Chinese girls, who is about nine or ten, starts clapping. She holds the palms of her hands straight up like cymbals and alternately brings one down onto the other. The rest of the group joins in. Each one moves differently, one swaying, one lifting and dropping his shoulders to the beat. The sax player slides off the car and holds the instrument out toward them while he plays. They start to dance around him. He hops up onto the sidewalk and the kids follow. He circles the car with the kids in tow.

"Gee, I really love ya, and we're gonna get ma-a-arried." A young black woman appears out of nowhere and is standing next to the car, singing. She has what sounds to me like a professional voice. The musician nods and smiles at her.

"Goin' to the chapel of love," she croons.

People on the sidewalk across the street stop and begin clapping too. A train goes by on the Manhattan Bridge directly above us. The kids are still dancing, the people are clapping, and the sax man is playing, but all I can hear is the train. After about thirty seconds, the noise subsides and I hear the sound of a guitar. The musician, with one foot up on the fender of the car, is playing a rhythmic accompaniment. He smiles at me.

"Nineteen sixty-four," he says.

The sax player comes up and stands next to him. They pick up the pace, and the people clap faster and faster. Finally, while the sax man is playing a string of cascading notes, the musician, strumming furiously, lifts his guitar handle into the air, then brings it down with a chop. They end at precisely the same moment. We all applaud enthusiastically.

"Let's go to a wedding," the musician says.

THE
MEANING
OF THE
WORD
DISCOUNT

The man raps on the door two times, once next to each lock.

"Change 'em," he says.

He nods in the direction of an old man who is sitting on a folding chair in the opening to the kitchen. "My father's got arthritis," he says. "When you're done, they gotta work smooth like butter."

He talks like Clint Eastwood and looks like one of the cops on *NYPD Blue*: short, fat, bald, and middle-aged. We are standing in the tiny vestibule of the apartment and his big potbelly squeezes me up against the wall at my back.

"I think I can handle that," I reply.

"Of course you can," he says. "You're a professional. That's why I hired you. I don't believe in hiring amateurs. You just end up paying for it later. I only deal with professionals. I'll spend more money for a professional because I know I'm gonna get good work. You know what I mean?"

"Absolutely," I say.

He narrows his eyes and stares hard at me.

"So how much did you say that was gonna cost?" he asks.

"Eighty dollars," I say. "Forty apiece."

"How about thirty?" the old man calls out.

The son smiles as he nods toward the old man. "I'll tell you what," he says. "How about we make it a nice round number like seventy?"

"I think eighty is a rounder number," I say.

The son laughs and looks at his father. "He drives a hard bargain, Dad. Whadya think? Eighty okay?"

The old man grunts.

"Okay. You win. Eighty," the son says. "But remember. Smooth, like butter."

I offer a thumbs-up sign and say, "Gotcha."

Finally, the son steps out of the vestibule and walks over to his father. "Lenny recommended him," he whispers to the old man, just loud enough for me to hear. "He *must* be okay."

"Do you have a license?" the old man calls to me.

"Yes, sir," I say.

"Don't worry. He's a professional, Dad," the son says.

I open the door and begin working on the bottom lock. The old man is watching me. I unscrew the cylinder and squat in the vestibule, preparing to repin it. Still his eyes are on me. I rummage through the little plastic container that contains my Allen wrenches, looking for the right size tool, and he says, "What the hell's he doing?" I look up, and now he is glaring at me, his left hand extended as if he's showing someone to a seat.

"Relax, Dad. He's changing the locks. I told you. Lenny recommended him. You remember Lenny. Jack's son. From the store on East Broadway."

The guy is standing behind his father now, his hands resting on the old man's shoulders.

"So why the hell is he taking so long? And what's he doing with that Tupperware container?"

"Dad. You gotta relax. I just told you. Lenny wouldn't have given me his name if he wasn't good. He's a pro. Let me get you something to drink."

"I don't need anything to drink, for Christ's sake."

The son walks a few feet across the living room to a chair and sits down. Then he picks up a newspaper from a side table and begins to read. I have finished repinning the first cylinder. By changing the pins to match new keys, I don't have to install a new one and can save the customer money.

"Dad? You see where Gotti got off again?" the son asks.

"Who?"

"Gotti? John Gotti."

"Who the hell cares about him?" the old man says. He is still watching me, his eyes never leaving my hands.

"Somebody must care about him. He's in the news every day."

The old man grunts again.

"Listen to this, Dad. Here's a guy who's a notorious criminal and all these people love him. They interviewed 'em out in Queens. They swear he's the greatest guy in the world. They say he pays for a big Christmas party on the block every year. That he takes care of his own." He jabs at the paper. "Here's a lady who says her son got hit by a car and Gotti paid for his entire rehabilitation. She thinks he's a god."

"So let her worship him," the old man says. "Makes no difference to me."

The son stands and walks toward the apartment door. He stops and leans up against the wall just behind me.

"What do you think of Gotti?" he asks me.

"Let him work," the father says.

I feel like a little kid, caught between the conflicting orders of his parents.

"He's working, Dad. He's a pro. He can work and talk at the same time. Relax." The son turns back to me. "Let me put it to you another way," he says. "Let's say you're a hospital administrator. Okay?"

"Why not. I could use a change of scenery."

"Everyone's a comedian," the old man says.

"Listen, Dad. Maybe you'll find this interesting." The son continues: "Okay. You're a hospital administrator. In fact, you're the top guy at this particular hospital. You call the shots. And some Mafia guy like Gotti comes to you and says that he's going to dump fifty million dollars in your lap to build a new wing especially for kids with cancer. But there's a catch. He wants it named after him. Big letters over the front door and on every floor. What do you do?"

The old man snickers.

I think for a minute and then say, "I do it."

"So it doesn't matter to you that the money that builds this hospital will have come out of the pockets of innocent people who have been ripped off, maybe even killed."

"It'll save lives," I say. "That's what's important."

"What do you think, Dad?" the son asks.

"A guy like Gotti doesn't give a damn about kids. Doesn't give a damn about anybody but himself," the father says.

I start to work unscrewing the top lock.

"You know," I say, "I saw the movie *Bugsy* yesterday. What you're saying reminds me a lot of Bugsy Siegel. It sounded like he was the kind of guy who would do something like that."

"Can you believe that, Dad?" the son says. "Is that funny? Is that funny or what?"

The old man is nodding his agreement.

"What's funny?" I ask.

"What's funny? What's funny, Dad? He wants to know what's funny." He walks over to his father and says, "My dad was Benjamin's doctor—that's what's funny."

I stop in the middle of my work. "You were Bugsy Siegel's doctor?" I ask.

"Benjamin," he growls. "Nobody ever called him Bugsy to his face."

This is, in fact, brought up in the movie.

"My father was almost everybody's doctor on the Lower East Side at one time or another," the son proclaims. "Two out of three people you see on the streets around here, my father delivered them. People were so grateful, he never paid for anything. He walks into any store on Essex Street, they still remember him. You don't know the meaning of the word discount till you've shopped with my father. He never paid for anything."

From the kitchen opening, the doctor rocks and murmurs, Greek chorus-like, "I never had to pay."

"Even with Jack and Davey," the son says.

"I never had to pay them anything."

"My father delivered Lenny," the son says to me.

Lenny's father Jack and uncle Dave started their lock supply business back when Essex Street was really Essex Street. They used to tell me stories about how they carried satchels on their backs and installed Segal locks for ten dollars. This was before even Bugsy's heyday, back when, as Jack used to say, "There were almost no Chi-niece."

"You remember when Dave came over that time in the middle of the night, Dad?" the son says. "Tell him about it."

The old man frowns. The son waits a few seconds and then

says, "One night years ago, my dad got mugged. Right, Dad? It was when you got mugged on Grand Street? What was that, twenty years ago?"

He waits again for his father to respond. Slowly, the old man rises and walks toward me. He moves in slow motion, dragging his feet forward in tiny steps. He stops in front of me, holds his hand up, palm forward as though preparing to pronounce a benediction, and coughs.

"It was one in the morning," he finally says. "I got mugged. My wife called Dave. She knew his wife, what the hell was her name? Selma maybe. He came right over. He brought a little bag with his tools. Like a doctor bag. I remember. I made a joke: 'Who's the doctor here?'"

The old man screws up his face. I smile. He stands next to me, swaying. It looks like he might just collapse against the wall.

"He changed the locks for me. When I asked him what I owed him, he just waved his hand." The doctor lifts his arm and flicks his wrist. His fingers brush the side of my arm. "'Forget it,' he said. 'I owe you.'" The son and father laugh in unison.

"No one ever charged him." The son jerks his thumb toward his father.

The doctor turns and makes his way back to his seat. I want to say, The guy got up at one in the morning for you. You should have paid him, you old fart.

Instead, I say, "Davey was a real craftsman. He taught me a lot about locksmithing."

The doctor lowers himself onto the chair and groans. I get back to work. I take my follower and remove the plug from the Medeco rim cylinder that Davey installed twenty years ago at one in the morning. Suddenly I feel weary. It is my first job of the day, but I'm already dragging from not enough sleep. My wife is eight months pregnant. She tosses and turns all night. When she is still, she snores, a side effect of the pregnancy. I end up on the couch and wake up with cricks.

Out of the blue, the son asks, "Do you use a computer in your business?"

"I'm sorry. What?"

"A computer. You must use one for your business, right?"

I put the last pin in and replace the plug. I slip the key into the tumbler. It turns, like butter, and I stand.

"Yeah," I say. "I have a computer."

"What kind?"

"IBM clone."

"What DOS you have?"

"I don't know. Four, or five. I don't really pay much attention to that. I don't use it for much."

"What do you mean, you don't pay attention? Why do you have one if you're not going to use it properly? You gotta pay attention. This is the kind of stuff that can change your life."

"Listen to him," the father says to me. "He knows what he's talking about."

"Seriously," the son continues, "with computers, little things can mean a world of difference to the average user. Take it from me. I'm in the business. You should get WordPerfect 6.01. Unbelievably better. Do you use Perfect? It's worth every penny. Check this out. Do you know what this is?"

He points to a large vertical box under the desk next to which his father is sitting.

"That's got everything. Right in there. There's the laser printer; there's the scanner. You like Scrabble?"

I nod. He suddenly scoots away to the back of the apartment.

"You're doing a good job on those locks, aren't you?" the father asks.

"Yes, sir," I reply.

"You bonded?"

"What?"

"Bonded. You bonded?"

Before I can answer, the son returns with a box in his hands. He removes a floppy disk and inserts it into the computer. He hits keys faster than an executive secretary, and the vertical box begins to whir.

"Watch," he says.

I finish screwing the lock on the door and look at the screen.

"Here," he says.

A Scrabble board appears. He hits more keys. He types letters. He asks the machine to play. The old man coughs and I look over to see that he is slumped back in his chair, tilting to the side.

"There. You see. The computer has found the word to make. Because. Because is the word."

"One in the morning," the father mumbles.

The son looks at his father, then me. "He's eighty-eight," he whispers. "Can you believe it?" He is nodding, agreeing with himself that at that age, anything is acceptable. "Just to be alive is gratifying enough," he says. He taps his right temple. "Starting to go. Just recently. That's why you're here. He can't remember things. Like where he left his keys."

He is interrupted by a loud noise. The old man has pushed his chair back and the legs have scraped against the floor.

The son rushes over to his father, helps him stand, and walks him into the kitchen.

"I just want a damn glass of water. I can do it myself," the doctor growls.

"Let me help you, Dad."

"For Christ's sake, leave me alone. I'm not going to fall."

For the past week, I have been helping my wife get up from the couch. I also make all the meals and do the shopping and the laundry. Her blood pressure is high. She is virtually immobilized. I go to work and wait for a message to appear on the screen of my beeper. THE TIME HAS COME. Whenever my beeper goes off, I wonder if the time *has* finally come.

While the two of them are in the kitchen, I pack up and write the bill. The son emerges and I hand him the keys.

"Okay," he says. "Let's do our business in the hallway. Back in a minute, Dad," he calls.

We step outside. He tries the locks. He removes his wallet and hands me four twenty-dollar bills. Then, deliberately, he dips in again and plucks out a ten. "This is for you," he says. I thank him. He walks me down the hallway to the elevator. An old woman is waiting there, her hands wrapped around the bar of a shopping cart. He pushes the down button, offers his hand, shakes mine, and says, "I'm sure you did a good job."

"I did," I reply.

"Good."

He walks back to his apartment, and as he is about to enter, he turns and says, "I'll call you if there's any problem." Then he closes the door.

I look at the old lady. She is less than five feet tall. Her skin is weathered and pouchy, dotted with brown age spots. She looks like a photo from a *National Geographic* article on any one of a dozen countries.

"Going shopping?" I ask.

"God willing," she says. She regards me for a second and then whispers, "You know it's a shame."

"Excuse me?" I say.

She glances down the hall at the apartment I just came from and jerks her head in that direction. "Can you imagine? He had to move home with his father. At his age."

"Really?" I say in disbelief. "What happened?"

"His life completely fell apart. Lost the wife, lost the business. The father's a saint," she says. "What he has had to put up with, with that boy, you can't imagine. I couldn't do it. Not me. Not in a million years. My son? Live with me again? Not in a million years."

The elevator arrives, and I hold the door until she wheels her cart inside.

"Got any kids?" she asks.

"No, but my wife's due in a month."

She presses the button for the first floor, and the door closes. "Congratulations," she says without enthusiasm.

CHICKENS,
LOBSTERS,
BUICKS

I am looking for Richard Nixon.

I'm on East Sixty-seventh Street, right off Central Park, waiting for a Miss Herrara to come out of her building. The man who answered the door said she'd be out in a minute, but it's already been five. I heard on the news today that Nixon just bought a townhouse around here somewhere, so I start looking for him.

It's a nice early-spring night. Leaves are blooming on the trees. I walk up the three-step rise to the sidewalk and check out the architecture. Four-floor buildings with small outdoor porches, French windows, iron gates with flower designs. A few feet away at the curb, next to a neatly stacked pile of black garbage bags, there is a small, wooden bookshelf. It is painted a deep shade of red and is in perfect condition. You can often find interesting things on blocks like this. Usable lamps, small appliances, sometimes a chair.

A car pulls up and parks across the street. Three older men in suits get out. They are laughing and acting drunk. They slap each other on the back, and one of them says loudly and incredulously, "She said what?" I step toward the street to get a better look. Maybe one of them is a former president.

"Mr. Locksmith?" a woman's voice calls.

I turn. A young woman with long black hair that hangs loosely to her shoulders is standing a few feet away. She is wearing a white blouse, a black jacket, and a short red skirt. Her earrings are little gold apples. Her lipstick matches her skirt.

"The car is down there," she says, pointing toward Madison.

She walks over to me. Even though she's wearing high heels, her eyes come up only to my chin. I am struck by how dark they are.

"Do you need me to be with you?" she asks.

I try to place her accent.

"Yes," I say. "I need that."

We cross the street and walk together to her car. Two of the three laughing men are standing on the sidewalk, smoking cigarettes. They cast glances at Miss Herrara.

"This is it," she says.

I am surprised to discover that it is a Buick. I had expected an Audi, or a BMW.

"Will this be difficult?" she asks as she opens the car door.

"Depends on what the problem is," I say.

"This won't go in." She holds up a round key, which I assume is for her Chapman cutoff lock. I take the key and examine it. She hugs herself and says, "I am a little cold. That is why I ask."

"I think this will be quick. If you don't mind waiting," I say. I get in the car and look at the Chapman lock. "No problem," I say. "It should only take a minute." I file off the small tab at the tip of the key. Then I insert it into the lock and realign it.

"There," I say. "That does it."

"Really? That is it?"

She steps up to the car and looks in. She is still holding her arms. She squats in the door opening and peers in at the lock. Her hair brushes my face.

"Mila said to call a professional," she says and smiles at me.

"Yes," I say. "It's always a good idea."

"Here. Can you start the car for me? Just to make sure?" She hands me the keys.

"Sure," I say.

I start up the car.

"Oh, how wonderful. And this will not happen again? It will be good?"

"Just make a new key and then throw this one away," I say. "You shouldn't have any trouble."

"Thank you. Thank you very much. Now I have to go back to the house to get my money," she says. "Please come."

I have decided on Argentinian. Maybe eighteen years old, no more than twenty. Maybe she works in the embassy, or she's an exchange student. In any event, she has that wide-eyed, fragile look of a foreigner caught in New York City's headlights.

We walk back to her house. The suited men are gone. As we approach her building, a young man wearing a black leather jacket and blue jeans passes us.

"*Buenas noches*," he says, nodding slightly at Miss Herrara as he goes by.

I look over at her. She nods at him but does not reply.

"Would you wait outside here, if you don't mind, while I get the money, please?" she asks.

"I'll go put my tools in the car," I say.

"Good. I will be right back." She enters her building.

Ten minutes later, when she hasn't appeared, I look in the first-floor windows, but the shades are drawn. I rap several times on the large brass door knocker. The sound echoes in the evening air. The same man I had encountered earlier opens the door.

"Excuse me," I say, "but I'm waiting for Miss Herrara. She said she was going to get some money to pay me."

He looks at me blankly. Finally he says, "So?"

"Well, she said she was going to be right out, but I've been waiting over ten minutes."

"I didn't see her," he says. "Maybe she's inside, but I didn't see her come in."

"Well, I know she's inside. I mean I saw her go in," I say.

"Well, you wanna come in and wait? You can wait inside if you want."

I step into a marble-floored vestibule. Straight ahead of me is a carpeted staircase, to my right a half-open door. The man motions for me to go through the door. I walk into a room about twenty by fifteen feet. There is a kitchenette to my right. A fat woman sits at a round Formica-topped table, smoking a cigarette and writing on a yellow legal pad. Her hair is pulled back and tied with a scarf. Behind her, there is a fireplace. In its interior is a rotating disc with a lightbulb behind it reflecting four different shades of red. In the far corner stands a five-foot, cream-colored ceramic Virgin Mary, her head slightly tilted. She is draped in cloth. A sectional sofa runs along the length of the wall to my left. It is flanked by a pair of three-foot purple vases filled with fake flowers.

The carpet is beige shag. The entire back wall is mirrored.

"Did Elizabeth come in?" the man asks.

The woman points toward the mirrored wall.

"This guy says she was going to get some money to pay him."

"For what?" She looks up at me.

"I'm the locksmith," I say.

"What'd she need a locksmith for?"

"Her car lock was broken. I fixed it."

She snorts. "Well, then she'll probably be out in a minute. She's probably doing something. Why don't you have a seat." She nods toward the sofa.

"Yeah. You can watch some TV," the man says. He sits down on the end of the sofa and picks up a remote. He flicks on the set and starts changing channels. He cranks the volume up very loud and then lights a cigarette. The woman punches numbers on a calculator and continues writing.

I sit down on the sofa and stare at the television, which is just to the side of the Virgin Mary's right hand. That's when I notice that there appears to be a door hidden in the mirrored wall. I turn to the man sitting next to me.

"Do you think you could possibly get Miss Herrara for me? I've got another job waiting," I say.

He points the remote at the TV and mutters, "Seen this one."

The woman looks up from her pad. "Don't worry," she says. "She'll be back. She's just busy for a minute."

Then she picks up the telephone and makes a call.

"Yeah, it's Mila. Yeah, I got your message. . . . No, I'm not ignoring you. . . . So what *do* you want? You think I'm a mind reader? You want chickens? Of course I've got chickens. . . . But what? *How* many? . . . What do you think, chickens grow on trees? You can't expect so many chickens without a wait. . . . They're coming, they're coming. . . . Oil is expensive. No! What world do you live in? You think you're going to get oil cheap today? Chickens, I can do something for you, but oil . . . Of course, my friend. Of course. Of course. Now what if . . . what? Lobsters? Lobsters I won't have until next month. *Next month*. What are you, deaf? Chickens and lobsters are two different things. . . . Because chickens are easier to come by. Lobsters are a different story. Listen. Be patient. Please. You have to be patient, my friend."

Mila is suddenly silent while she listens to the voice on the other end. Throughout her speech, the man next to me hops from one program to another, resting on one for no more than ten or fifteen seconds.

"Look," Mila continues, "chickens are seventy-five. Where do you think you are going to get such a price? Lobsters are . . ." She stands and hits buttons on the calculator. "What are you talking so much for? Listen to me a minute. How many lobsters do you want? . . . Oh, so now it's oil again. I'll tell you what. I'll give you the chickens for sixty-eight if you take the lobsters next month. . . . Yes, I'll make it a big shipment for you. Will that make you happy? Of course I want to make you happy."

On the TV, some crook blows away a cop. I stare into the fireplace. Every once in a complete cycle, a tiny piece of red light falls on the Virgin Mary's face.

"Excuse me. I hate to bother you again, but I really have to get going. Is there anything you can do to see if she is back there?" I jerk my head toward the door in the mirrored wall.

The man looks at me. He is now apparently annoyed. He turns back to the TV. He has decided on the cop show.

"Can't help you, guy," he says.

Mila slams down the phone.

"Idiot!" she screams. "Why do I have to deal with such idiots?"

I walk over to her. The yellow legal pad is covered with numbers.

"Mila? Do you think you can get Miss Herrara for me?" I ask.

Mila glares at me.

"Why don't you sit down, my friend," she says. She motions to the chair across from her and moves the things on the table onto the floor by her feet. "While we're waiting, let's talk."

"Look," I say. "She only owes me fifty bucks."

"Please," she says. "Sit."

I sit.

"Now. Why don't you tell me about yourself?" she says.

"Excuse me?"

"Talk to me. Do you like your work? Are you married? Do you have children?"

"I don't think—"

"Don't be embarrassed," Mila says. She laughs. "Men are always so embarrassed to talk. You might not believe this, because you look like an intelligent young man, but men almost always—" She holds her fingers up to her mouth and zippers it closed. Then she reaches over and pats my arm. "Come on. Tell me a little bit about yourself. I'm sure she'll be out in a minute."

I look at the door in the mirrored wall. There is no door-knob, only a tiny semicircular wedge carved out of the glass for a fingerhold. From my place at the table, I can hardly tell it's there. "Well," I say. "I like my job. Especially when I get paid."

"Good. That wasn't so hard, was it?" she says, ignoring my sarcasm. "Do you ever wonder why it is sometimes so hard to say even the little things? Perhaps there are other things, things under the surface, things that aren't so good, things that make it hard for you to talk. Let me see your hand. Some people think I can read the future. Here." She reaches across the table and takes my wrist. She pulls my hand toward her. With her finger she traces the lines.

"I see that you not only like your job but that you will always like it. That you will do well in it."

"That's good," I say.

"But I see other things. Things that are not such happy things."

She folds my fingers up and slides my hand back.

"Like what?" I ask.

"It is better not," she says. "I certainly do not claim to see everything, but I often see things clearly, things that others cannot see. Sometimes these things are not pleasant."

"What? What do you see?"

She looks again at the palm of my hand and sighs.

"Love," she says. "There are many problems with love. Problems that will take years to make better. You have hardships in store for you, my friend. And here. Look." She shows me the course of a long line running diagonally across it. "Here, where it splits. This means you also have a health problem to worry about."

She releases my wrist and pushes my arm back across the table.

"I am going to do something for you," she says. "I know it is not necessary, but I want to because you seem like a nice, intelligent young man who understands that life is not always what it appears to be. Am I right, my friend, that you can see that clearly?" Without waiting for an answer, she reaches down and pulls a small packet out of the bag at her feet. "I am going to give you these herbs. You must keep them with you always. And tonight I will light a candle for you. I will light the candle and say prayers. And then every night, for the next week, I will light another candle for you. This is very special."

"Thank you," I say.

"You're welcome. Good luck to you, my friend."

Mila stands up. I stand up. It occurs to me that I am now being asked to leave.

"That's very kind of you, Mila. The candles. And the herbs. I was wondering, would it also be possible for you to pay me the fifty dollars Miss Herrara owes me and then she can pay you back?"

The man on the sofa gets up and walks over to the kitchen table. Mila holds out her hand. Then she reaches down and retrieves her calculator.

"Let's see," she says. "Each candle is nine dollars. The herbs I will throw in for free. You seem like such a nice young man. That's seven candles at nine. Sixty-three. I'll tell you what. I'll cover the fifty for the girl, and I'll just forget about the difference. We'll call it even."

The man walks over to the front door and opens it. He stands there like a butler, waiting for me. Mila smiles and says, "I think now you should get out of here."

"You know, Mila," I say, "I think Richard Nixon's going to fit very well in this neighborhood."

As I walk out the door, she yells after me, "You know you got a deal, you jerk. The herbs are worth a hell of a lot more than the candles."

WHAT
WE
NEED
TO
KNOW
ABOUT
FORGETTING

"It's around here somewhere," Dr. Hunter says, squinting into the distance.

We are walking down Ninety-first Street between Fifth and Madison Avenues, searching for his car. I look through the first-floor windows of the house to my right and see a large crystal chandelier hanging over a dining room table. In the next building, there is a white tufted bird sitting on a trapeze swing inside a six-foot-tall cage.

Dr. Hunter sees me looking. "Beautiful, don't you think?" he asks.

"Yes," I say.

"I can't remember what it's called," he says.

"It's a cockatiel, I think," I say. "My five-year-old daughter is really into exotic birds. She has lots of books about them."

"That's wonderful," he says. "I'm not very familiar with birds myself. Sarah knew birds."

For a moment, I forget about his car and we stand there observing the bird.

"I don't know if it's a talker," I say.

"I'm not a big fan of talking animals," he says. "I prefer pets that don't act like people."

Dr. Hunter is a short, thin old man who appears to be in good physical shape but has a bad memory. I, however, find it less than significant that he can't remember where he parked his car. I often have to park blocks away from my building and must rely on a handmade street map drawn on a bulletin board next to the front door of my apartment. I use a pushpin for my car and the first thing I do upon entering is shift the pin.

"So what kind of car do you have, Dr. Hunter?" I ask.

"A Chevrolet," he says. "An Impala."

"An Impala? What year?"

"Nineteen sixty-nine." He laughs. "Just like me. Vintage."

I begin searching for an old Chevy Impala.

"I bought it originally for my son when he went to college. He gave it back to me a couple of years ago when Sarah and I got the country house. Sarah's not his mother. His mother was never interested in country houses." He laughs again. "Nor Chevrolets, for that matter. She was more the BMW type. She used to try to convince me to buy a BMW. She said that it was more of a doctor's car. My *son* bought a BMW after he gave the Chevy back to me. Which makes sense because he is more his mother's type. A big spender. What do I need a BMW for? That's what I told her years ago and I told him the same thing, which is why he gave the Chevy back to me."

He puts his hand on my arm.

"It runs great," he says. "If we ever find it, you'll see."

"Maybe it's on another block," I say. "I'm always forgetting where I park my car."

"I told my son when he gave it back to me that it

made a beautiful kind of symmetry. That was the very word I used. Symmetry."

"What color is it?" I ask.

He raises his shoulders and his head drops slightly into his neck, as though it's rubber. He momentarily squints up at the sky. "I'd . . . say . . . it's . . . green. Although there's a lot of gray in it." He chuckles and looks down at the sidewalk as he walks. "It's actually what they used to call hospital green. Appropriate, don't you think? For a doctor to drive a hospital green car?"

I can see no old Chevy Impalas anywhere near Madison. I start walking in the other direction, toward Fifth. Dr. Hunter follows me.

"Is that it?" I ask. I point toward the other side of the street. "On the right. A couple of cars in from Fifth Avenue."

We walk toward the vehicle. He peers intently now in that direction. "Yes," he says. "I do believe it is. And I was certain I had parked near Madison."

We cross the street and stop next to an old gray-green Chevy Impala with an M.D. license plate. There are several dents in the body and many small pieces of paint missing. I choose the passenger door to work on because it is curbside. I slide my Slim Jim between the window and rubber stripping. The button pops up instantly. At that moment, an old beat-up Mustang screeches to a stop in the middle of the street next to us. A man bursts out and yells, "DON'T MOVE!" He is holding a small gun with both hands on top of his car. The gun is pointed directly at my nose.

"HANDS UP, BUDDY. UP."

Dr. Hunter and I raise our hands.

"DON'T MOVE. STEP BACK TWO STEPS. KEEP YOUR HANDS UP."

We do so and then I ask, "Are you a cop?"

His right hand quickly dips into his jacket pocket and produces a police badge, which he extends forward across the top of the car.

"Well, I'm a locksmith," I say. "This gentleman has lost his car keys."

"Not exactly lost . . ." Dr. Hunter says, but is cut off by the cop, who yells, "DON'T MOVE, AND SHUT UP!"

The cop walks around his car and comes toward us.

"You got identification?" he barks at me.

"Yes. In my wallet. I carry my license in my wallet," I say.

"Take it out very slowly," he says.

I remove my wallet and then my locksmith license and show it to the cop. He glances at it and immediately lowers the gun. "Okay. You can put 'em down now." Then he turns and looks over the car. "Your car, Pops?"

"Yes," Dr. Hunter says.

"What year is it?" He is now all smiles.

"Nineteen sixty-nine," Dr. Hunter says.

"Hey. My Mustang's a '68." He pats Dr. Hunter on the side of the arm. "Do you have the registration?" the cop asks.

"It should be in the glove compartment," Dr. Hunter says.

"Why don't you get it?"

The doctor opens the door and pulls a stack of papers out of the glove compartment. He places the pile on the hood of the car and sorts through it.

"Here it is," Dr. Hunter says. "A bit crumpled. But readable."

He hands it to the cop.

"Thanks," the cop says. Without glancing at the registration, he takes me by the arm and walks me a few feet away. He says, "Sorry if I scared you, buddy. There's a lot of car theft in this neighborhood. Even in broad daylight. These guys are gettin' ballsier every day." He lowers his voice and makes a circular motion with his head. "When these people around here complain about something, we've got to put on a show of force." He puts his gun into a chest holster.

"Okay, Pops. Drive careful," he says and hands Dr. Hunter the registration. Then he gets back in his car and speeds off.

"Well, that was quite unusual," Dr. Hunter says.

"Yeah. Just like television," I say.

"Actually, I don't watch television, but it's very much like what I imagine television to be," he says.

I grab my tools and slide into the front seat of the Chevy. I notice that the button on the driver's side door is up. It was open all along.

"Could your keys be somewhere in the car?" I call.

"I guess that's possible," he says.

I search the interior but find no keys.

"I'll have to replace the ignition cylinder," I say.

"Whatever it takes," he says. "You're the doctor."

It's an old car, so I don't have to break down the entire steering column. I install the new cylinder quickly and start up the engine. It sputters and rattles but doesn't stall.

"What a wonderful sound," the doctor says.

I shut it off and get out of the car. Suddenly I am overcome by dizziness. A huge spasm courses through my body and I think I hear a distant explosion. I have to hold on to the door to keep from falling down. Dr. Hunter places his hand on my shoulder.

"Deep breaths," he says. "Deep, slow breaths."

I lean against the car, waiting for my head to clear. When I no longer feel faint, I let go.

"Why don't we go back to my office and I'll pay you there," he says.

He holds his hand against the small of my back as we walk to his building.

"Now I know what they mean when they talk about how it feels to stare down the barrel of a loaded gun," I say.

"I used to work in a prison," Dr. Hunter says. "I've seen guns many times before. They often have this effect on people who are not used to them. The fear often comes after."

He holds the door for me, and we enter the lobby. His office is the first door on the right. There is an oval brass nameplate affixed to it. LEONARD HUNTER, M.D. is written in script.

"Why don't you sit down. Here." He moves a pile of books from a chair onto his desktop. "Would you like a glass of water? Nature's elixir, you know."

"No, thank you," I say. But as I sit, the dizziness returns and I immediately change my mind.

Dr. Hunter walks into the back room, and I hear the sound of water running from a faucet. I look around the room. An entire wall of floor-to-ceiling bookcases of dark, walnut-colored wood is to my left. I am sitting in one of two armchairs opposite his desk. They have upholstered backs surrounded by a wooden border and wooden arms with small upholstered sections in the middle. An old oil painting, a country landscape, is hanging on the wall to my right. There is a brass picture light above it. The huge desk occupies the space in front of the two windows, which are largely obscured by thick, floor-length burgundy curtains. There are piles of books and medical journals on the floor in the corners.

I notice a flier sitting on the edge of his desk. I reach forward and take it. At the top of the page is the title, WHAT

WE NEED TO KNOW ABOUT FORGETTING. Written on an angle underneath, as though on an invisible flag fluttering in the wind, is the subtitle, *When Should I Worry?*

"Here you are." Dr. Hunter returns and hands me a glass of water. Even in the semidark, I can see a grayish brown cloud swirling around in it.

"That's a workshop I'm attending at church," Dr. Hunter says. "Keeps me busy."

I replace the flier. I wait for the cloud to disappear and then take a sip. Remarkably, it tastes wonderful.

"Never needed to keep busy when Sarah was around. This, by the way, is Sarah." He hands me a small framed picture from the other side of his desk. "Never a wasted minute with that woman. *Lively* doesn't do her justice. She also kept me in line. She always knew exactly where I put things. Including car keys," he says, looking up at me and flashing a little smile.

The black-and-white photo is of an older woman with shoulder-length gray hair, sitting on a park bench, leaning forward, her forearms resting on her knees. Her head is tilted up very slightly and her expression is one of mild embarrassment. Her face exudes kindness.

"Feeling any better?" he asks.

"Yes," I say.

I stand and stretch.

"Don't push yourself," he cautions. "You can rest here as long as you like."

He is wearing reading glasses. He leans his head forward and scans the desktop.

"Looks like you've been in this office for a long time," I say.

"Forty years," he says.

I get up and slowly walk over to the bookcases. For a second, the image of the gun pointed at my face crosses my mind and the dizziness returns. I concentrate on the bookcases and the way they are constructed. They are not store-bought but quality craftsmanship, built into the space by someone who knew what he was doing. Medical books, most of them psychology texts, line the shelves. I read the titles, one after the other.

"Psychiatrist?" I ask.

"Yes."

"Still practice?"

"Only up here." Dr. Hunter laughs, tapping the side of his head.

I met a parade of psychiatrists in the years after my brother got sick. Dr. Hunter doesn't seem like any of them.

"Do you mind if I ask you a question?" I ask.

"Not at all," he replies.

I pause, unsure of what to say next. "I have a friend," I say.

"Yes. Many of us do," he says.

"Yes."

"And your—friend," Dr. Hunter says, "is he not well?"

"That's right. He is not well."

"How is he not well? Or should I say, how not well is he?" He removes his glasses.

"He is very not well and it depends on whose opinion you're getting as to why."

"Is he psychotic?" Dr. Hunter asks.

"According to some people, yes. Paranoid schizophrenic. But there have been a few who labeled him manic-depressive."

Dr. Hunter nods. He holds out his hand for me to sit. I walk back to the chair.

"He's a very bright man," I say.

"Yes. There are very many bright men who are ill mentally."

"He was a philosophy professor and he suffered a sudden nervous breakdown almost fifteen years ago. He never recovered. He goes in and out of hospitals and—uh—his parents basically support him. He's in a vicious cycle. He's totally unproductive and he just can't seem to break out of it. It's almost as though his former life is meaningless to him. As though he doesn't want to be who he used to be."

"You mustn't think he is choosing this for himself," Dr. Hunter says.

"Maybe not, but it's unbearable for those of us around him. Watching someone you care about so . . . helpless."

"I know that this type of situation is most painful," he says. "You must know that there is no solution, no obvious solution, ever. What is your question?"

"My question?"

"Yes. You started by saying you wanted to ask me a question."

I finger the frame of the picture of Sarah, which I am still holding.

"Well, I guess my question is whether in your opinion, this type of condition is ever reversible after so many years. Is it conceivable to think that if he stays alive, somehow, through the grace of God, that someday he might recover, at least enough to function relatively normally?"

Dr. Hunter gets up and walks around the desk. He stands in front of me and speaks in a completely different voice from the one I had been hearing.

"This," he says, "is what I believe. You are walking down a road. And you come to a hill. You look up the hill and realize that you have to walk up it. You don't know why. You don't stop and think about why. It is simply there to be climbed. It is steep, but you are determined. You take your first step and begin. At first you do not believe it will be possible to succeed, but eventually you gain momentum and allow yourself to hope. Suddenly there looms a figure ahead, coming down the hill toward you. It is an ominous figure and you cannot quite make out who it is. You only know that it frightens you and as you draw closer, you decide that the only way you will ever make it past this figure and onward up the hill, is to kill it. You approach it. At the moment you raise your arms to strike down the stranger, you realize that it is your father."

He stops his speech suddenly. His arms are poised above his head. His eyes are fixed on my face. We stay in that position for several seconds until he lowers his arms and says, "I have not practiced formally for several years. But you can tell your . . . friend . . . to call me. I do not think I would like to take on his case, but I would be glad to talk with him if he likes."

He walks slowly back around the desk, removes a business card from his wallet, and hands it to me.

"Now, let's see about writing you a check," he says.

He opens a drawer. He bends over, peers inside, and then closes it. He opens another.

"I know that checkbook is around here somewhere."

"Sarah would know," I say and hand the photo to him.

He takes the picture and looks at it. "Yes," he says. "Sarah would most certainly know."

STORY
VALUE

Moosie is waiting for me in front of the green peppers.

"I'll be in my office, Joe," he had said over the phone this morning. "By the vegetable stand. Heh-heh."

I watch him for a couple of minutes from the corner of Bayard and Mulberry Streets. He's short, fat, and bald. He's wearing baggy old jeans and a dirty white T-shirt. He stands at attention and keeps looking left then right, left then right. He is the only person around who isn't Chinese, but the workers at the vegetable stand act as though he isn't there. One of them sits on a chair directly to Moosie's left and wraps bunches of grapes. Others zip in and out with boxes on their shoulders.

"It's fireworks season, Joe," Moosie had said over the phone. "I need a really good locksmit in fireworks season."

Moosie wipes the sweat off his forehead and scratches his large stomach. He pushes his glasses up his nose, but they immediately fall down again. He reaches over, takes a couple of grapes, and pops them in his mouth. I start to cross the street and before I reach the other side, he calls to me.

"Joe?"

"Yeah. Moosie?"

We meet in the middle of Bayard Street.

"Hey. I knew you must be Joe." He leans toward me. "Not many of us around here, you know what I mean? So how you doin'?"

"I'm good, Moosie," I say. Saying his name out loud makes me feel a little silly. We shake. His hand is sweaty.

"Listen. I need you to do me some good locks, Joe. Bobby said you were the man for the job."

"Bobby?" I ask.

"You know, Bobby. From the restaurant up on Mott."

"Oh, sure," I say. "I remember Bobby."

"Come on. Follow me."

We walk back to the vegetable stand.

"You want an apple, Joe?"

He reaches over to a pile behind me and tosses one in the air. I catch it. "They got good stuff here," he says. Then he whispers, "Come on. Let's do some locks."

He walks quickly to the other side of the vegetable stand and disappears down a stairway.

"Joe. Come on. It's safe," he calls.

The opening is so narrow that I have to carry my tool bags in front of me. My shoulders brush the brick walls on either side. At the bottom, the alley is dark and everything is covered with bird shit.

"You okay, Joe? It's kind of hard to see down here. Come on, it's right over here."

I follow him to the end. The alley opens up to a width of about ten feet. On one side, there is a large metal box, which appears to be a compressor, and a new steel door at the back wall.

"This is it, Joe."

Moosie opens the door and steps inside. He flicks on a light.

"I want ya to make it strong for me, Joe."

"Sure, Moosie. I can make it as strong as you want."

"Great," Moosie says. "As long as it keeps the fuckers out. Hey, c'mere, Joe."

I step into a tiny boiler room. A small furnace is on the right. Piled up against it are dozens of boxes. Each one is labeled in black Magic Marker. ROMAN CANDLES. M-80'S. CHERRY BOMBS. PINWHEELS. THUNDER BOMBS.

"Pretty nice, huh?" he asks.

I nod.

"Now you see why you gotta make it strong."

"Yeah," I say.

"This is my favorite," he says. He opens the flap of the box next to him and removes a package.

"Flying Color Butterfly Rocket," he says. "These Chinese guys really know how to name their stuff, huh?"

"Listen, Moosie, can I ask you a question?"

"Sure. Go ahead. Ask anything you want. But I already know what you're thinkin', Joe, and you don't have to worry about a thing. We've been sellin' out of this place for years. I was born in this building. I used to play in this room when I was a kid. That's my writing over there."

He points to a spot on the wall behind me. I see nothing but bricks.

"This place is in the family, you know. My mother and father moved here just after they got married. My uncle and aunt lived across the hall till he died. She moved to Jersey, but she still talks about comin' back here. Says she's dyin' in the suburbs." He walks over to the door. "So whadya think?"

I turn and look back down the alley. I can barely hear the street noise.

"What about this?" I point to the boiler. "Aren't you worried this might explode?"

"Explode? Heh-heh. I wish the fucking thing would explode. Maybe they'd fix it and we'd get some decent heat this winter." He steps over to the door and closes it. "This thing isn't on, Joe. It's June. It's fireworks season. Now, come on, you gotta make this strong. I got a lot of stuff here to protect. And the bastards are gonna come after it. Okay?"

Someone knocks at the door. Moosie says, "Who?"

"Victah," a guy says.

Moosie opens it.

"Hey, Victor, this is Joe, the locksmit. He's gonna do us some good locks."

"Good to meet ya." The guy extends his hand and we shake.

Victor is over six feet tall, wide shoulders, muscled. He is wearing a white sleeveless undershirt. His chest and shoulders are covered with hair.

"Gonna keep the fuckers out, Moose?" he asks.

"What do ya say, Joe? We gonna keep the fuckers out?"

"Yeah," I say. "Depending on who the fuckers are."

They both laugh.

"Here, Moose." The guy hands over a wad of bills. "I need six more."

"You see any trouble?" Moosie asks.

"Nah."

"Good. Come back when you need more."

Victor leaves and Moosie turns to me.

"So how much I owe you, Joe?"

"I haven't done the job yet, Moosie."

"That's okay. That's okay. I want to pay you now."

"Okay," I say. "Ninety-five."

He hands me a hundred-dollar bill and then peels off a ten from a large stack.

"You do me good, Joe, and I'll do you good. You know what I mean? This bein' fireworks season, I always need a good locksmit. I'll be upstairs in my office when you're done. Heh-heh."

He leaves and I unpack my stuff. I make my marks on the door. I am now dripping with sweat. There is no electrical outlet, so I unscrew the lightbulb and install my adapter. I plug my drill into it. There's a little popping noise across the room and then a steady low, hissing sound. I quickly jump away. There are more mechanical noises. I peer around the furnace and see a small hot water heater, which has just sprung into action.

This, I say to myself, is the last job I do for Moosie.

Three days later, I meet Moosie again at his office.

"You won't believe what they fucking did, Joe," he says, motioning for me to follow him. We head down into the alley, where Victor is waiting for us.

"Look at this, Joe," Moosie says.

There is a six-inch hole in the door where the lock used to be. Jagged pieces of steel stick out away from the surface.

"Can you believe these guys?" Moosie says.

Victor laughs. "At least they waited a couple of days, Moose."

Moosie takes a banana out of his back pocket and peels it.

"So," he says between swallows, "what can you do for me here, Joe? We gotta get this back into shape."

I stare at the hole in the door and think about the conversation I had with my wife this morning.

"I don't think you should go back there," she said.

"What are you talking about? The guy's a big teddy bear," I replied.

"I just have a feeling, Joel," she said. "I don't think you should do another job for this guy."

"Why not?"

"Well, for one thing, selling fireworks is illegal."

"Yeah, but it's way down on the list," I said. "Next to jaywalking."

"You hate it when people jaywalk," she said.

"So whadya think, Joe? Maybe two or three locks?" Moosie asks. He is eating fruit salad now out of a small plastic container.

"Moosie. Whoever did this could probably destroy the whole door if they wanted to. We're talking good money after bad here, I think."

Moosie wipes his mouth on his arm.

"Shit, it's hot. Fucking June heat waves. Nothin' worse than a June heat wave. Some years it's nice and cool. You go out on the street and sell all day and hardly break a sweat. Last couple of years . . . Shit, you think it's really that's ozone layer stuff, Joe? All this heat?"

"I heard it was that volcano, Moose. The one in Mexico," Victor says. "Fucked up the atmosphere."

"There ain't no fuckin' volcanoes in Mexico. You're thinkin' about Mount Saint Teresa or whatever the fuck it was."

"No, Moose. I think it was Mexico. The thing blew last year."

Moosie makes a face. He's either trying to remember about the volcano or wondering how he could have ended up with an assistant like Victor. Finally he turns to me.

"What do you think, Joe?"

"I think Victor's right," I say. "It was Mexico."

"I'm talking about the fuckin' door! Jesus. Who gives a fuck about Mexico?"

Victor suddenly has a serious look on his face and I begin to wonder whether my wife was right.

"So. What do you think? Two, maybe three of 'em?"

"Two's enough," I say.

"Okay. Two. But you gotta cover the hole somehow."

"I guess I could get some sheet metal," I say. "And put one lock here and another way down low if you want."

"Sheet metal! That's it, Joe. What do you think, Victor? Sheet metal?"

"Sheet metal's good, Moose," Victor says.

"And I like one down low. But not too low. I can't bend like I used to."

"Yeah, you're too fuckin' fat, Moose."

Moosie turns to me. "You know, if I didn't know this guy since I was able to beat the shit out of him, I'd get somebody to beat the shit out of him. Low like here, you mean?" He taps the door at thigh level.

"Sure," I say.

"Great," Moosie says.

"Will it slow the fuckers down?" Victor asks.

"Yes," I say.

"Great," Moosie says. "Let's do it. How much do I owe you, Joe?"

"I don't know. Why don't you pay me for this one when I finish?"

Moosie points his plastic fork at me.

"Can I trust you, Joe?" he asks.

The thin, white tines are pointed right at my eyes. I try to make a face like I'm thinking about the answer to his question. Finally I say, "Sure." He laughs loudly and lowers his utensil. Then the two of them head back down the alley.

At the end of our conversation this morning, my wife said, "So tell me the truth. Why are you really going back there?"

"I don't know," I said.

But as I measure the door for how much sheet metal I'll need, the real answer to that question suddenly occurs to me. "For the story value," I should have said.

The heat wave is now eight days long. It's eight-thirty in the morning and it's eighty-two degrees. A group of Chinese guys is unloading fish packed in boxes of ice into the store next to the vegetable stand on Bayard Street. Old ladies are holding tiny umbrellas over their heads. A man standing next to me, waiting for the light to change, says to his friend, "Thank God we got the Fourth of July weekend. I don't think I could stand another day on the subway in this heat."

Moosie appears suddenly behind me.

"The fuckers did it again, Joe."

Moosie is breathing fast. His glasses are hanging on the very edge of his nose.

"Same way?" I ask.

"Worse. They destroyed the whole door. I had to get a new one. These guys are costing me a lot of money. Last night, I hear them smashing at the door, yelling, 'Moosie, you're gonna have to get a new door, Moosie.' Laughin' their asses off. Woke up the whole building."

We cross the street and stop in front of the vegetable stand. Moosie coughs a few times and takes a peach from the pile in front of him. A Chinese man with a large box of lettuce hoisted on his shoulder yells something unintelligible at him.

"The heat's even gettin' to the Chinks," Moosie says.

"Didn't anybody call the cops?" I ask.

"What?" Moosie says.

"When the guys were breaking down the door. Didn't anybody in the building call the cops?"

Moosie begins chuckling to himself.

"That's a good one, Joe. That's really a good one."

We descend into the alley. When we reach the bottom of the steps, he is laughing out loud. He laughs so hard that he doubles over and then coughs until he regains his breath.

"Moosie?" I ask.

"Yeah, Joe?"

Peach juice is running down his chin.

"Can I ask you a question?"

"Sure, Joe."

"Why are you going to pay me to put more locks on this new door when these guys are probably just going to do the same thing all over again?"

"I'm going to give them a key this time, Joe. Maybe this time they'll just take some of it."

"Oh," I say. "You're going to give them a key."

"I don't know what else to do, Joe. This year's been bad. Really bad. Maybe the heat's got those guys too. They never been this bad before. Come on."

At the end of the alley there is a brand-new door.

"One more time, Joe," Moosie says. "Something simple."

"Moosie. Are the cops the ones breaking down your door?" I ask.

Moosie gives me the same look he gave to Victor during the volcano discussion. Then he says, "You didn't get that?"

"I'm a little slow, I guess."

"Who the hell did you think it was, Joe? They're just doin' their job. The guys upstairs say go out and bust up the fireworks guys. So they go out and bust me up. They got a special fireworks squad. They do this every year. 'Cept this year's been bad. Really bad. Maybe the heat's got those guys too."

"So let me get this straight. Now you're going to give the cops a key?"

"Yeah. I figure maybe if I give them the key, they won't bust me up and maybe they'll leave some stuff behind."

"So if the cops are the ones breaking down the door and now you're going to give them a key, why are we bothering to put a lock on the door at all, Moosie?"

Moosie smiles and says, "To keep the fucking Chinese bastards out. That's why. Not so complicated, huh?"

"Guess not, Moose," I say.

"So whadya say? One more time, Joe."

Moosie steps into the boiler room. He pulls a bag of grapes out of the box labeled CLUSTERING BEES ROCKET. Then he leans up against the boiler.

"You know, Joe, when I was a kid, this neighborhood was half Italian. There's hardly any of us left now. The fucking Chinese have taken over. They are the toughest people I ever met," he says. "All business."

He comes out and sits on the ground in the alley.

"If you don't mind my asking, Moosie," I say, "how'd you ever get into selling fireworks?"

Moosie laughs.

"How'd you ever get into bein' a locksmit, Joe?"

"It's a long story," I say.

"Yeah," he says, "me too."

He offers me some grapes and I reach down and take a few.

THE
NAKED
CITY

The guy on the car radio says the wind-chill factor is thirty-five below. I wipe the inside of the windshield clear with the palm of my hand. The defroster can't keep up.

"Friends," he says, "if you don't have to go out, don't."

I have to. It's my job.

I am driving down Fourteenth Street. It's ten o'clock at night. The N in the red neon sign of Julian's billiard parlor is out. The pool hall has switched genders. There's a line in front of the Palladium. This absolutely confirms my belief that at any time of day, regardless of the conditions, there is, somewhere in this town, a line.

"It was eighty-three degrees in L.A. today, kiddos," the radio guy says.

I flash my middle finger at the dashboard.

"Yeah," I say, "but they never get real winter there."

"Why don't you all just take your clothes off, settle into a nice warm bath, and spend the night with me," he says.

I cross Third Avenue and spot a parking space across the street. A quick U-turn and I park right in front of my destination. Small favors. I take a deep breath, turn the engine off, and step out into the arctic blast.

"I got crack, I got 'ludes, I got reefer."

A tall dark man bundled up in a coat and a hooded sweatshirt is standing in the doorway. He is bouncing in place to keep warm.

"What you need, man?" he asks.

"I need you to move so I can buzz," I say, trying at the last second to make it sound like a request.

He steps slightly to the side.

"I got somethin' here will warm you right up," he says.

I find the right button and press it. I haven't taken my eyes off the guy. There's a buzz and I push the door open.

"Maybe somethin' on the way out," the guy says.

"Yeah. How about a cup of hot tea," I say.

I start walking up the stairs. He yells after me, "Lemon or milk?"

On the fourth floor two art posters are hanging on the wall, a Cézanne still life and a Gauguin Tahiti scene. They are attached with pushpins. In between them in a two-by-three-foot wooden frame is a dingy old painting, a surrealistic landscape, Escheresque. It shows a pier jutting into a body of water, with a line of pilings that evolve into trees and eventually transform into monsters. A small, lone figure is standing out at the edge of the pier, staring off into the mist. I look at it for a while. Then I find the right door and knock. After a few seconds, I knock again.

"I'm comin'," a gruff voice says. "Jesus."

The door opens, and a totally naked, very old man is standing in front of me.

"Yeah?" he asks.

I stare at his face.

"I'm . . . a locksmith," I say.

"No shit?" he says. "I'm a brain surgeon. What can I do for you?"

He looks like Popeye. He's bald and his cheeks are puffed out. His chin is a tiny U that hangs beneath them.

"Who's there, George?" a voice calls from inside.

The man turns his head and I quickly look at the rest of his body. He is rail thin. His skin sags off his skeleton in small, folded layers from his chest down to his waist, as though he's melting.

"Who the hell'd you say you were?" he asks, turning back to me.

"Locksmith," I say.

"He says he's a locksmith," George calls over his shoulder.

"Let him in, George. I called him."

George takes a step back. "Jesus," he says. "Nobody tells me anything."

I step into the kitchen, a space about about ten feet square. On the other side of the room, leading to the front of the apartment, is an archway filled with hanging strands of purple glass beads. Dishes are piled up next to the sink. There are two frying pans and two saucepans on the stove top. It smells like a wonderful meal was just cooked. Just to my right, the valve at the top of the radiator is hissing loudly. The moist, intense warmth of the room feels great.

George closes the door.

"I'll be with you in a minute," the voice calls from the other room. I hear more voices, all men, and the clicking of what might be poker chips.

George is smoking a cigarette now. He leans back against

the counter and blows perfect smoke rings up into the air. I can see the veins in his legs. He reaches over and picks a string bean off one of the plates and pops it into his mouth. He takes a puff while still chewing.

"They never tell me anything," he says to me.

I make a knowing, empathic face.

On the wall over his shoulder is a painting much like the landscape out in the hallway. In this one, a chain of mountains gradually metamorphoses into devil-like creatures spitting fire down on a few deer, which are leaping away in the lower right-hand corner.

"Well, now, thanks for waiting."

A second naked old man walks through the beaded archway.

"And thanks for coming out on such a brutal night," he says.

He has the opposite physique of George. A large potbelly, flabby thighs, lots of body hair. What is going on here? I wonder.

"Nobody ever tells me anything, Frank," George says. He sounds sad, almost hurt.

"Oh, don't be ridiculous, George. I told you three times I called a locksmith. I almost couldn't get in tonight. What happens if you have another stroke and we can't get in? You want us to just let you die?"

"Yeah, George," someone calls from the other room, "use your damn head and stop being so sensitive. Come on back and finish your cake."

George grunts and turns on the faucet. He holds his cigarette under the flow, then flicks the butt into a bag next to the table.

"You guys are worse than my wife," he says and walks through the archway into the other room.

Twenty minutes later I am finished with the job. I call out, "All done." There's no answer. They're listening to music in the other room. Mozart, I think.

"Fellas? I'm finished."

"Just come on back," a voice answers.

I'm reluctant to venture any farther into an apartment filled with old naked guys, maybe cradling Satan dolls or sacrificing chickens. But finally I decide that since they are so old, maybe even octogenarians, they are harmless. Why they are walking around naked is a mystery.

I put on my coat and step through the beads. I'm in a dark bedroom, large enough only for the mattress and a night table. There is another archway, this one beaded in yellow, and I step through that into a small office area, where there is a desk with a computer on it, a file cabinet, and shelves full of books.

"Keep coming," the voice says.

One more crossing, green this time, and I have traversed the railroad apartment into the caboose, a dimly lit living room. The fat man is sitting on a couch between two more naked ancient men. George is in a chair to their left. They all have the bored looks of people at the end of a long city council meeting. I lay a set of keys on the coffee table in front of them.

"Six, right?" the fat man asks.

"Six," I say.

"Excellent. Want some cake?"

"That's okay, I—"

"Try it," he says, holding out a plate toward me. "William made it." He tilts his head toward a fifth naked senior citizen standing over by the window at the end of the room, holding a record in his hands. He is enormous, much larger than the fat man on the couch. He has a full head of shiny white hair and a thick beard.

William nods and smiles at me.

"It's a torte," he says.

"William worked for years as a pastry chef," the man to the fat man's left says. "It's excellent."

I decide that even if they all descended on me at once, I could probably escape the apartment with little difficulty. I accept the plate.

"Sit down." The fat man motions for me to use the chair at my elbow.

"I don't mind standing," I say.

"Please. There's another chair here," William says.

I sit.

They are all staring at me. Except for George, who is slumped in his chair, nodding off. I look around the room. It is neat and orderly, the furniture worn but intact. There are two small paintings on the wall over the couch, done in the same style as the others.

The fat man sees me looking. "George did those," he says.

"Years ago," William adds. "In his dark period. Before Carol."

"We all believe he would have made it had he kept at it," the fat man says.

"Absolutely," the man to the fat man's left says.

William nods.

I take a bite of the cake. It is delicious.

"Coffee?" the fat man asks.

"Why not. I'll have some coffee."

"Milk and sugar?"

"Just milk."

He pours it for me and hands it across the table.

"William was just about to put on some more music. Do you like Mozart?" the fat man asks.

"I love Mozart," I say. "This is very good, by the way." I point my fork at the cake.

"Told you," the man to the left of the fat man says.

The music begins. The fat man pours more coffee for himself. He lifts the pot and offers it around to each of his friends. No one is interested. George has fallen asleep in his chair. The fat man puts down the pot and whispers to the group, "I think he's doing remarkably well."

"Me too," William says. He carries the extra chair over and places it down between me and George, closer to me. He says, "He's a tough old guy. He'll be okay."

We listen to the Mozart. I sip my coffee. The fat man's eyes are closed while he holds his coffee cup in front of his mouth. He hums lightly along with the music. William is staring at George. The other two men look like lifeless wax figures.

After a minute or two, William says, "What's your schedule like tomorrow, Fred?"

"I've got to take Betty to the doctor's in the afternoon," he replies. "I'm good for the morning."

"Why don't you just sleep here, then?" the fat man says. "That would be easier. It's so damn cold out there."

"Nah. I'll just come back. Betty doesn't like to wake up alone. George'll be all right. I can get here around nine."

"I'll take the afternoon," William says.

"Good," the fat man says. "What about tomorrow night? Fritz?"

The man to the fat man's right nods.

"I'm free all day Wednesday," the fat man says. "That covers it until Thursday. We'll work out the rest of the week by phone."

There is a prolonged silence during which they all appear to become absorbed again in the music. Then William turns to me and asks, "Are you married?"

"Yes," I say.

"Wonderful. Kids?"

"Yes. Two girls."

"Wonderful. How old?"

"Eight and one."

"Cherish them."

"I will. I do."

"All of us here are grandfathers," he says. "Fred has a four-year-old great-granddaughter, I believe."

"Six," the man on the fat man's left says.

"Six already." William shakes his head. He looks at me and says, "It goes so fast. Before you know it, it's over." He leans toward me and whispers, "George's wife just died. We're keeping him company."

The fat man suddenly struggles to his feet and says, "Speaking of wives"—he steps out from behind the coffee table—"I told Emmie I'd be home by midnight." He walks across the room and opens a closet door.

"Henpecked," the man at the end of the couch says. It is the first thing he has uttered since I entered the room.

George lets out a series of snores. They all laugh. The fat man comes over to me and hands me some money.

"Thank you," he says. "Stay warm."

I stand. Everyone else except for George also stands. I realize that I have stopped wondering why they are all without clothes.

THE
GOİNG
RATE

"Could you explain this to me one more time?" she asks. "I'm just not very good with numbers."

"Okay. No problem. My service charge is forty-five—"

"That's for what you've done so far? Just for opening up the door?"

"Right. So far, you owe me forty-five."

She furrows her brow and nods.

"And what's the extra charge you were talking about?"

"That's if you want me to replace the cylinder. That's twenty-five extra."

"Twenty-five?"

"Yes."

Again the nodding.

"That seems like an awful lot. I mean, if the first charge is forty-five, it makes more sense to have the second charge be something like fifteen. I mean, I'm not in business. I don't really know very much about these kinds of things, but that would make more sense to me."

She stares right at me as she talks and does this little thing with her lip and eyebrow for emphasis.

"I know it may seem like a lot," I say, "but believe me, I'm not trying to take advantage of you or anything. That's the going rate."

"Well, it may be the going rate, but it still seems like a lot to me," she says.

She walks to the table in the foyer. Her shoe heels click on the parquet hardwood floor. She looks into her purse and counts the money in her wallet. I have been standing in the doorway since I drilled the cylinder and let her into the apartment. I watch her from there. She's early thirties, with shoulder-length brown hair, wearing an expensive two-piece maroon suit and black patent leather shoes with brass adornments. Her small breasts are concealed by the suit. She has no ass, zero sexuality.

"I just can't deciiiide," she whines.

"Would you like me to decide for you?" I ask.

"Excuse me?"

"I mean, do you want my opinion?"

"I don't think that was called for," she says.

"I didn't mean anything by it. I just—"

"I'm sure I can make up my own mind."

"I'm sure you can. I was just wondering if there was anything I could say that would make it easier. I wasn't trying to insult you."

"I wish people would be more conscious of how they sound," she says. "It would spare the rest of us a lot of pain."

I wonder what she knows about pain. The Sutton Place digs, the Madison Avenue clothes. I could tell her a thing or two about pain.

"You know, you really have a tone-of-voice problem," she says. Her lip and eyebrow do that dance again. "You sounded like you were insulting me. You may not acknowledge that, but it was as clear as day to me."

I usually make a habit of being polite, of maintaining a professional relationship, of respecting the fact that I have entered my customer's private world. But this morning I got a fifty-dollar parking ticket, I now have three jobs waiting for me, two of which I am already late for, and I need to speed things up a little. So maybe my tone of voice was a little curt.

"I'm sorry," I say.

"It's okay," she says. "No problem. I accept your apology."

Suddenly a police helicopter swoops down out of nowhere and circles the building across the street. The noise is intense. The two of us watch it until a minute later it turns south and disappears.

"That was really strange," I say.

"What's so strange about it?" she asks. "That's New York City. Your living room window is just as entertaining as your TV set."

"Well, I don't think that a police helicopter hovering outside your window is something you see every day. Especially in this neighborhood."

"This may be Sutton Place," she says, "but it's still New York City."

She steps into the kitchen, and I hear an aluminum can being opened and liquid poured. She returns holding a tall, thin, cobalt blue glass.

"You know," I say, "you've got another lock. You can get along without replacing this one for now. Maybe the super can do it for you."

"The super's an idiot."

"Well, it's not a real difficult job. Maybe he can do it and he probably won't charge you as much. If you change your mind, just call me back."

"If it's not such a difficult job, why are you charging me twenty-five dollars to do it?"

She takes a sip.

"I'm a professional," I say. "Professionals get paid more."

She seems satisfied by that.

"If I decide to call you back tomorrow, will you do it for twenty-five?"

"Well," I say, "no. Then I would have to charge you forty-five because that's my minimum service charge."

"Well, that's totally unacceptable!" she cries. "Then you'll just have to wait until I decide."

She strides off down the hallway toward the bedroom. I feel somewhat shell-shocked and try to mentally reconstruct this interaction, hoping to find the hidden door out of it.

After a minute, she calls, "If you replace it, will I get the same lock, the same kind of lock that was there before you came?"

Her voice sounds soft and polite now, as though she is making a concession. I congratulate myself on the assertive strategy. Firm but fair, like dealing with my eight-year-old.

"Yes," I respond, "the same kind."

"The exact same kind?" she calls again.

"What do you mean?" I ask.

She appears in the hallway, pauses for a second, and then walks back into the living room.

"What do you think I mean? I mean, the exact same kind. Same shape, same color, same—"

"Yes. The exact same kind."

"What was the old one?"

"Excuse me?"

"What kind was the old one?"

"I'm not sure," I say.

"Well, where did you put it?"

"There." I point to the table in the foyer.

She picks up the old cylinder, which I had placed on a copy of *The New York Times*.

"This is a"—she holds it up in front of her face—"Yale. So you'll replace it with a Yale, right? For twenty-five dollars?"

"Actually, I don't have any Yale cylinders with me. I would replace it with an Ilco, which is comparable to—"

"But I thought you said it would be the *exact . . . same . . . kind*."

I look out the living room window at the giant Pepsi sign across the river in Queens. I wish I was in Queens right now, doing a job for some construction worker's wife, listening to her curse at herself because she broke the key off in the lock. She'd yell and pace and pout and then *pay me to replace the cylinder*.

"You're right," I say. "It's not the exact same lock. It's a very high-quality, *comparable* lock. And if you would like to pay me twenty-five dollars, I'll install it for you in your door. If you wouldn't, I'll just pick up my bag of tools and head on out of here."

The phone rings.

"Excuse me for a second," she says and lifts the receiver off the wall unit next to the opening to the kitchen.

"Hello? . . . Oh, hello. . . . I'm fine, Robert." She lowers her voice and steps halfway into the kitchen. "No. I can't talk now. . . . Yes, business. . . . No, I'm not lying. Why would I lie? That was your specialty. . . . Oh. Excuse me for insulting you. That is so unkind of me. Almost as unkind as you screwing around behind my back. . . . Snide? You're calling me snide? . . . What? What for? What possible reason could you have for wanting to get together with me?"

I am uncomfortable standing in the doorway in such close proximity to this conversation. So I walk across the living room and look at the photographs on a bookcase shelf. One is a picture of the woman in cap and gown standing in between an older couple, probably parents. Another is her next to another woman out in a park, arm in arm, with big smiles. Then there is one turned facedown. I lift it. It is a wedding picture of the woman with her husband. They are in profile, both laughing. Each is holding a piece of cake in front of the other's face.

"I'd prefer it if you didn't touch that," the woman says.

She is looking at me from the edge of the foyer, arms folded in front of her. She looks like she's been crying. I put the picture down.

"Now. Where were we?" she asks.

"We were talking about Yale cylinders," I say.

"Oh, yes, that's right. Yale cylinders. You'll have to forgive me. I'm feeling a little . . . I just don't have a lot of experience at this. At making decisions like this. It wasn't my . . ."

She looks down at her right hand, which is clenched in a fist. She opens her fingers. The Yale cylinder sits in her palm.

"Silly me," she says and bursts into tears.

"Look. It's okay," I say. "You don't have to decide anything right now. If you want me to come back tomorrow for twenty-five dollars, I will."

She turns her back to me and wipes her cheeks with her fingertips. When she has composed herself, she turns back and asks, "Why the sudden change of heart?"

"Let's just say I know how tough it is," I say.

"Do you? How tough what is?"

"What you're going through."

"Really?"

"Yes," I say.

"And how do you know what I'm going through?"

She stares at me with tears in her eyes.

"I'm really sorry," I say. "But it'll get easier. It will."

She reaches into her jacket pocket and pulls out a fifty-dollar bill.

"Here," she says.

I step toward her and take it.

"I don't really think this is any of your business."

She turns and walks to the door. She opens it and waits for me to leave. I pick up my tools. As I pass her and step out into the hallway, she says, "I appreciate your offer. I'll call you if I need you."

She closes the door.

Years ago, when my girlfriend Deborah walked out, my friends took care of me. I slept on Kenny's living room floor; Michael brought me meals; Gary made sure I didn't walk in front of any speeding vehicles. We were engaged, not married, but the hurt's the thing. The hurt is what you remember.

I walk down to the elevator and push the button. It takes forever to arrive. Minutes go by. An apartment door down the hall opens and closes. Just as the elevator arrives, the woman turns the corner. I wait for her to enter, then I get in. She pushes the lobby button and the door closes.

I stare at the illuminated number panel above the door. We are on the seventh floor when she says, "You know, I'm not accustomed to being talked to like that by a service person."

TRUE
FRIENDS

"I knew it was you," the old man says.

He is about five-foot-four, with a thin ring of snow white hair around the lower half of his head. He taps a finger against his temple. "I saw you from a block away and I said to my wife, 'That's him.'" He turns to the short, thin old woman standing behind him. "Didn't I say that's him?"

Her arms are folded in front of her. A pair of glasses hangs from a cord around her neck. She takes a step back on the sidewalk away from the front door of the store.

"I asked myself, what would he look like, what would the man look like who is going to save our day, and just at that moment, just when I had developed, so to speak, that picture in my mind, boom, there *you* were, crossing the street with a bag over your shoulder, and I said, 'That's him—there he is.'"

He extends his arms up like a circus performer who has just completed his act. He has not stopped smiling since I arrived.

"And you were right," I say enthusiastically. "Here I am."

He peers more closely at my face. "You know you're actually a lot younger than I expected."

The woman snorts.

"I have a baby face," I say.

"Char-lie," the woman says.

"Right. Down to business now." He takes me by the arm. "Here is the patient." He points to a scratched and dented doorknob lock.

"Looks like you've been exerting a little force here," I say.

He turns to the woman and laughs. "Force? I think I'm a little too old for such a word. Maybe ten years ago force. Right, dear?"

"Twenty," she says. "Let the man do his work, Charlie."

"Of course, dear, of course. Just a little chitchat." He holds up his hand in the shape of a duck bill and flaps his fingers up and down onto his thumb. "It's such a beautiful day. I don't want our little misfortune to spoil this glorious afternoon."

She reaches forward, takes him by the arm and tugs.

"May I see the key?" I ask.

The man shrugs. "Unfortunately, I cannot comply with that request," he says. "I don't have even the slightest idea—"

"We never had a key," the woman interrupts.

"That's right," he says. "We've been here for over thirty years and never once locked that lock. When we first took over the store, they gave us a big ring of keys. I never even bothered with them. I threw them in a drawer and that's where they still are. Right in that desk back there."

He jabs his finger toward the door, indicating a piece of furniture surrounded by boxes in the rear of the store. The woman lets out a big sigh.

I remove my pick set from my bag and lay several different rakes on the ledge of the window to my right.

"Okay, now we're going to see some real action," the man

says. He twists the invisible dial of a combination lock, first one way, then the other. "Safecracker stuff. Do you mind if I watch you operate?"

"Not at all."

I lubricate the cylinder. Then I slip the tension bar into the keyway and hold my thumb down on it. I insert a rake and rock the pins. In less than a minute, the tumbler turns. I use a small screwdriver to rotate it the rest of the way and the door opens.

"Amazing," the man says. "Simply amazing. Just like on television."

The woman brushes past us into the store and calls, "Charlie." Charlie picks up one of the rakes and runs his finger along it. "They look like dental tools."

"I guess they do," I say.

"That's my business." He points to the front window of the store. Painted there in now-faded gold are the words AMSTERDAM DENTAL SUPPLY.

"So how did you do that so quickly?" he asks.

"That's *my* business," I say.

"Of course it is." He laughs. "So what do we do about preventing this from happening again?"

"We put in a new lock with a key that you don't put on the big ring in your desk drawer."

"A wonderful idea," he says. Again he taps the side of his head. "You may be as smart as me."

Charlie and the woman are working in the back of the store. She stands behind the desk, glasses on the end of her nose, hitting buttons on an old-fashioned electric calculator, while he lugs stacks of large books off shelves and deposits them in piles in front of the boxes that encircle her. Every few minutes, Charlie says something like, "Invoices from '88, dear" or "Insurance records, sweetheart." Then the woman grunts and says, "By the bathroom" or "That stack there." Old dentistry catalogs litter the floor and I notice on one of the upper shelves behind me a row of plaster casts of full sets of teeth. Six four-drawer file cabinets, each with a piece of paper taped to the top handle with the word EMPTY written in big black letters, stand side by side to my right. It seems as if they are closing up shop.

Charlie appears next to me. "You know, you really look like you know what you are doing." He wipes his forehead with a handkerchief. "The way you opened that door before, and now the way you are handling those tools. I can tell that you are a true craftsman."

"Thank you," I say.

"I was born in Poland. There were so many good craftsmen in Poland. It was always a pleasure to watch them work."

"My grandfather was born in Poland," I say.

"Really? Was *he* also a craftsman?"

"Actually, my Russian grandfather was the craftsman. My Polish grandfather became a businessman."

"Do you happen to know what town in Poland your grandfather was born in?"

"Yes. It was called Drawhubbich. I think I'm pronouncing it right. It was in an area called Galicia."

"Ah, Galicia." He nods. "I know Galicia. Good Jews came from Galicia." He sits down on a small stack of boxes and stares out the window. "Are you Jewish?" he asks.

"Yes."

He nods and says, "I was in Poland during the Occupation." I wait for him to continue, but he simply sits there and stares at the traffic outside as if he has forgotten my presence. The sun comes out from behind a cloud, revealing the swirling dust particles in the air. The scene reminds me of one of those winter wonderland glass balls filled with water and white flakes. The sun slips back behind the cloud and the dust particles disappear. Charlie says, "We used to do minesweeping back then. Do you know how we did it?" The far-away look is still in his eyes, but he is smiling now.

"No," I say. "How?"

Charlie scoots off the boxes. Then he places his hands over his ears, closes his eyes, and suddenly begins to jump up and down. Puffs of dust rise off the floor as he pogo-sticks around the room. "Like this!" he calls. "This is how we did minesweeping!" At that moment, his wife walks up to him and places her hands on his shoulders, forcing him to stop.

"Ethel. I'm telling him how we did minesweeping in Poland," he says, gasping for breath.

"Sit down and rest," she says. "It's too hot for this kind of activity."

"That is how we did minesweeping," he says to me over her shoulder.

Charlie sits and Ethel walks around the counter that runs the length of the far side of the store. She squats and opens drawers. She removes some folders, places them on top of the counter, and glances back at him.

"What a day this has been," Charlie says. "You know, while we were trying to open the door, we got a ticket on our car right out there on Amsterdam. We were standing no more than twenty feet from the car. The lady could see us in the doorway, but she gave it to us anyway."

"Happens to me all the time," I say. "They always tell me they're only doing their job."

"You should be careful you don't get a ticket," he says.

"I have some friends waiting in my car for me."

"Ah, that's good. It is very important to have good friends."

He removes his handkerchief from his shirt pocket, wipes his forehead, very deliberately folds the cloth into a square, and replaces it.

"Let me tell you a story about good friends," he says. "In Texas, there are rattlesnakes. Large rattlesnakes. And this business group went out for a picnic." I lean up against the door and watch him tell the story. "So. A young man who worked for the business asked his boss, 'Boss. What am I going to do if a rattlesnake bites me?'"

Ethel crosses between us, carrying file folders.

"Ethel. I'm telling him about good friends."

"So finish telling so you can get back to work," she says. She returns to her post at the desk and resumes punching numbers on the calculator.

"Okay," he continues in a slightly lower voice. "So the boss told the man, 'If a rattlesnake bites you, you've got to suck out the poison.' And the man asked, 'But what happens if the rattlesnake bites me on my ass?' And the boss looked at the man and said, 'Well, then you'll know who your true friends are.'"

I laugh.

"That's a good story, right?"

"Yes," I say.

"I love a good story," he says.

"Me too," I say.

Charlie slides off the boxes. He takes a deep breath and puts his hand on his hip like he has a crick in his side, but he keeps his eyes focused on my face.

"You know, if you like good stories, you should read Isaac

Bashevis Singer. He writes great stories. He was Polish, you know."

"I know. I have read him."

"Really? You have?"

"Yes."

"That's unusual, I think."

"What is?" I ask.

"To find a working man who reads somebody like Singer." He looks at me a little apologetically, then adds, "At least in this country."

"I've always loved to read, ever since I was a kid," I say.

"So what kinds of books do you like to read?"

"Oh, just about everything. But I like novels and short stories the best."

Charlie looks at me intently, as if I am an old acquaintance he has not seen in years, someone he once knew well, in another life.

"You know, it seems to me that you must experience many stories in this job you do."

"Yes, I do. Lots of them," I say. "Sometimes I even write them down."

"I knew it!" he exclaims.

"What?"

"You're a writer," he says.

"Well, I try," I say.

His face takes on a look of exultation. "That is wonderful," he says as if I have just announced my engagement to his daughter. I am unsure how or whether to react to this congratulatory sentiment. He turns to the back of the room and calls, "Ethel. Ethel."

The sound of the calculator stops and in an annoyed voice Ethel says, "What?"

"The locksmith. He is a literary man."

Charlie walks over to the door and places his hand on my arm. "Are you finished with the new lock?"

"Yes."

"Come back here for a minute, please." He leads me to the rear of the store and retrieves a folding chair, which he sets up next to the desk. He waves to me. "C'mere. *You* would appreciate this. My wife is something of a writer. More than something. She is a fine writer. Sit down. I want you to listen."

"Charlie," Ethel says. Her voice, for the first time since I arrived, is soft. "Charlie, we have so much work to do."

"And we will tomorrow and the next day. Just take a minute, dear. He will appreciate this. He writes himself. Excuse me."

Charlie reaches past Ethel and opens one of the desk drawers. He removes a hard-backed folder. He pushes the calculator to the side and centers the folder.

"Sit down, sir." He motions toward the chair. "Sweetheart, please. You sit too."

Ethel sits in the desk chair. Her face looks completely different now, more like a reticent schoolgirl's than a humorless old bookkeeper's.

"My wife is special," Charlie says. "She was in Auschwitz. That doesn't make her special. There were many in Auschwitz. But *she* has written about it. She has a gift for words."

"Charlie."

"It's true, my dear. Don't be modest."

"I have simply told my tales," she says.

"Tales that others would not tell," he replies. "Could not tell. Tales that you had to tell for them." Charlie leans over the edge of the desk and says to me, "Listen."

Ethel takes a deep breath and opens the folder. She turns several pages and says, "This one will do." She looks hesitantly up at me and for a second I think she is going to reconsider. And then she begins to read.

Her voice is flat and unemotional. Her words are simple, but they paint clear, perfect pictures. She reads slowly, as if it is a new piece and she is trying it out on me. Charlie's eyes are closed. Every few sentences, he nods and murmurs.

In the story, Ethel is a young woman on a boat sailing into New York Harbor. As she sees the Statue of Liberty for the first time, she recalls the members of her family who died during the Holocaust. She describes each person, what he or she looked like before the war began, their talents, ambitions, what they meant to her. Then she details their deaths, the ones she saw and the ones she could only imagine. " 'They should all be here with me now,' " Ethel reads. " 'I will never forget them.' "

When Ethel finishes, Charlie is in tears.

"She read that at a United Nations rally," he says. "In front of hundreds of people."

"That was a long time ago," Ethel says.

"Read the one about Miriam."

Ethel finds the piece and reads to me about a young girl who died in the camp. Miriam was eight when she fell ill and Ethel gave her food from her own meager portions. Ethel was eighteen and had already lost her own younger sister. " 'It was just as painful when Miriam died,' " she reads. " 'How beautiful she was, even in death, even with her pale, cracked skin and her protruding bones.' "

Charlie hands her another sheet of paper from the folder and Ethel reads a piece about her first impressions of America.

When she is finished, she says, "That's enough. The writer is done reading."

"You see what I mean?" Charlie asks.

"Yes," I say. "That was wonderful. Thank you, Ethel."

"You're welcome," she replies. "Now, Charlie. Can we get back to work, please?"

Charlie slowly gets up and lifts Ethel's chin with his fingers. He kisses her on the cheek. They stare at each other for a few seconds and then he resumes the task of transferring and sorting the boxes of old records.

"Do you have a bill?" Ethel asks me. "I'll write you a check. You better get this money while it's still in here." She taps the checkbook with a pen. I hand her the bill, and she writes out a check.

"Here." She holds it in her extended hand. "Take this too." She gives me a manila envelope.

"What's this?" I ask.

"It's nothing. Something to pass on to someone else who might appreciate it."

I thank her and say good-bye to the two of them. Charlie vigorously shakes my hand and says, "It's been a pleasure."

On my way back to the car, I think about the two of them, a dental supply selling team. After all they had lived through, they still miraculously have things to be thankful for.

My two friends are waiting for me impatiently.

"What the hell took you so long?" Jim asks.

I get in and take out Ethel's story. "Listen to this," I say and begin to read.